The Super-Delicious
Slow Cooker
Recipe Book UK

1500-Day Simple Slow Cooker Recipes to Help You Share With Your Family
the Cuisine of France, India, the USA, and Other Countries

Kristine Chambers

CONTENT

69 ❯ Chapter 6 Soup, Chili and Stew

85 Chapter 7 Desserts

97 Conclusion

98 Appendix Recipes Index

Introduction

A slow cooker is an electric device that cooks food for a long time at a low temperature.

Slow cookers are excellent for breaking down and tenderizing big chunks of meat like pot roasts or beef stews because of this low-and-slow technique. But they have other options as well. A home cook's preferred method for making soups, ribs, dips, beverages, and bread is the slow cooker. In addition to its adaptability, a slow cooker has a lot of additional advantages, such as the ability to uniformly prepare food without needing to use your hands. Home chefs may now conduct other household chores, run errands, or start their day in the office because of this. Additionally, slow cookers are simple to use and typically only need to be plugged in. Simply turn on your slow cooker, add the ingredients for your selected meal, adjust the heat to low or high, depending on the recipe's directions, cover it, and let it simmer. If you don't want to consume your meal right away, you may either keep it warm in the slow cooker or turn the slow cooker off to turn off the heating element. I'm done now! For some dishes, such as ground beef chili or pork chops, it is necessary to brown some of the ingredients in a pan before adding them to the slow cooker. You might want to think about preheating your slow cooker in these circumstances.

Fundamentals of the Slow Cooker

What is Slow cooker?

A slow cooker is a type of cooking vessel that is frequently constructed of porcelain, metal, or ceramic. Typically, a heating element-containing electrical unit completely encircles it. The pot's bottom or all of its sides may have a heating element. A typical version is a straightforward metal heating plate with no edges at all, on which your cooking pot rests. All of them feature a glass, metal, or ceramic cover. These covers are intended to provide a low-pressure seal that keeps moisture within the pot. Food within the pot is cooked as a result of heat rising the pot's sides from the electric base. While cooking, slow cookers maintain a low, stable temperature. Nowadays, the terms "crockpot" and "slow cooker" are interchangeable. If your hectic schedule prohibits you from being in the kitchen before mealtime, a slow cooker is an answer. Dinner may be prepared in a slow cooker and left to cook while you are away from home. The typical slow cooker tends to consume less energy than an oven, even if it must be left on for several hours.

How to Use Your Slow Cooker?

Slow Cook Low and High:

1. Put the cooking pot into the main housing of the appliance. To turn the device on, plug it in and hit the power button.

2. Fill the cooking pot with the ingredients. Put a cover on the saucepan.

3. For LOW or HIGH, use the SLOW COOK button. The button's default setting is HIGH. The button will change to WARM if you press it once more. It may be changed to LOW by pressing it a third time. It will cycle back to HIGH if you press it a fourth time. NOTE: On the High setting, the default time on the temperature/time display is 4:00, and on the Low setting, it is 8:00.

4. To set the time, press the TIME button once. To change the time, use the Up button, and to reduce it, press the Down button. The time may be changed in 15-minute intervals from 12 hours to 30 minutes.

5. The cooking cycle will begin 3 seconds after the cooking time has been selected.

6. While the food is cooking, the timing can be changed. When selecting your initial settings, press the TIME button and then utilize the Up and Down arrows.

7. The device will beep three times and then switch to Stay Warm for up to 12 hours when the countdown timer hits zero. As an alternative, you can push the Power button to halt cooking before the allotted time has passed (the unit will NOT switch to Stay Warm in this case).

8. Press the Power button to turn the device off when you are ready to do so. The Temp/Time display will show the word OFF.

Warm Function:

1. Put the cooking pot into the main housing of the appliance. To turn the device on, plug it in and hit the Power button.

1. Place the hot, cooked food in the pot and secure the lid. NOTE: Do not overfill the pot beyond two-thirds.

1. Select SLOW COOK from the menu. The default setting is HIGH. To pick WARM, press the button once more. NOTE: On the Warm option, the default time on the temperature display is 6:00 (hours). Using the Up and Down arrows, you may change the time in 15-minute increments up to 12 hours.

1. The warming cycle will begin 3 seconds after you pick WARM.
1. While the food is cooking, the timing can be changed. When selecting your initial settings, press the TEMP/TIME button and then utilize the Up and Down arrows.
1. Press the Power button to turn the device off when you are ready to do so. The word OFF will appear on the temperature/time display.

Benefits of Using Slow Cooker

Unattended meal preparation. The main benefit of using a slow cooker is for safe, simple unattended cooking. Keeping food warm at parties and events.

Saving money: A stove or oven consumes far more energy (kWh) than a slow cooker. A slow cooker won't heat your house as well as larger equipment will if you live somewhere with hot summers.

Of course, dining at home is less expensive. Low-and-slow cooking is ideal for inexpensive meals like slow cooker beans or difficult meat cuts like beef chuck roast and hog shoulder. However, these inexpensive items are simple to prepare on a stovetop or in an oven.

In addition to cooking in a wet environment for a prolonged length of time, slow cookers attain a simmer temperature of 209°F, which safely eliminates common pathogens including E. coli, salmonella, and botulism.

What Can You Cook in a Slow Cooker?

A slow cooker can be used to prepare almost anything. You're probably most familiar with the hearty slow-cooked soups, stews, and main meals that benefit from boiling for hours on ends, such as chili, meatloaf, pulled pork sandwiches, and shredded chicken tacos. Dinnertime is also made simple with one-pot meals like casseroles cooked in a slow cooker.

Popular slow-cooker side dishes include baked potatoes and vegetable dishes since they take place in your oven for the main course. Additionally, attempt to cook softer veggies like peas, spinach, or zucchini later in the process.

There are a few surprising uses for your slow cooker that you might not be aware of. Hashbrowns, oatmeal, and even cinnamon buns may be prepared in the slow cooker for hands-free breakfast and brunch meals. A party can also be prepared in advance with the help of slow-cooker appetizers like fondue or cheese dip. Try a slow-cooker spaghetti dish instead, but watch out for gritty pasta by not letting it simmer for too long.

Also, savory dishes don't have to be cooked in slow cookers. Cakes, puddings, candy clusters, and other sweet treats may be made with these slow-cooker dessert recipes. You can even treat yourself to a sweet slow cooker beverage, like hot chocolate or tropical-infused tea.

Instructions for Cooking

Pasta and Rice

• If you're converting a recipe that calls for raw pasta, macaroni, or noodles, cook them on the stovetop for a brief period until they're just barely soft before putting them in the slow cooker.

• When substituting raw rice for cooked rice in a recipe that asks for cooked rice, add ¼ cup more liquid for every ¼ cup of raw rice. For the best outcomes, while cooking continuously all day, use long-grain converted rice.

Beans

• Beans must be properly softened before being combined with sweet or acidic meals. Beans will not soften because of the hardening action of acid and sugar.

• Red kidney beans, in particular, should be cooked before being added to a dish. Bring to a boil three times as much unsalted water as the beans in a separate pot. Boil for 10 minutes, then lower the heat, cover the pot, and simmer the beans for 1 ½ hours, or until they are soft. If desired, soaking in water should be finished before boiling. After boiling or soaking, discard the water.

• Beans that have already been fully cooked can be used in place of dry beans.

Vegetables

• Low cooking temperatures and slow cooking periods enable many vegetables, especially those with roots, to fully develop their flavors. In contrast to cooking them in the oven or on the stovetop, they don't frequently overcook in a slow cooker.

• Put the veggies in the slow cooker before the meat when making recipes that call for both roots vegetables and meat. In a slow cooker, rooted vegetables often cook more slowly than meat.

• To make cooking easier, place rooted veggies close to the stoneware's bottom or sides. Mix in the sliced or chopped veggies along with the remaining ingredients. You should parboil or sauté the eggplant before putting it in the slow cooker since it has a very strong taste.

Herbs and Spices

• Hearty, fresh herbs like rosemary and thyme hold up well for meals with shorter cook times. Fresh herbs enhance flavor and color when added toward the end of the cooking cycle. Many fresh herbs' tastes will fade over extended cooking durations if used at the beginning. Use sparingly, taste toward the conclusion of the cooking cycle, and add the proper seasonings, including salt and pepper, if necessary. Ground and/or dried herbs and spices work well in slow cooking and may be added at the beginning. It is usually advised to taste the food and make any necessary seasoning adjustments right before serving because the flavor intensity of all herbs and spices can vary substantially based on their strength and shelf life.

Liquids

• Always make sure the recipe calls for a proper amount of liquid to achieve the best results and avoid food from drying out or burning.

• Always fill the stoneware to a minimum of 12 full and a maximum of 34 full, and follow suggested cook times.

Milk

• Milk, cream, and sour cream break down during extended cooking. Add in the final 15 to 30 minutes of cooking, if at all feasible. Milk can be substituted for condensed soups, which can also cook for a long period.

Soups

• Two to three quarts of water are needed in certain soup recipes. Then, only enough water to cover the other soup ingredients in the slow cooker. When serving, add extra liquid if you like a thinner soup.

• Add 1 or 2 cups of water to milk-based soup recipes that call for no additional liquid during the first cooking process. When the cooking cycle is complete, gently whisk in the milk, cream, or sour cream because they will curdle if heated past the boiling point.

Meats

• Trim the fat from meats, thoroughly clean or rinse, and then pat them dry with paper towels. While adding more flavor depth to the meal, browning the meat in a separate skillet or broiler enables fat to be drained off before slow simmering.

• Adjust the number of veggies or potatoes if you choose a smaller roast so that the stoneware is ⅓ to ½ full.

• Always keep in mind that the specified cook time and meat size are only approximations. The unique cut, meat arrangement, and bone structure of a roast will determine the precise weight that can be cooked in a slow cooker.

• When preparing meat with pre-cooked beans, fruit, or lighter veggies like mushrooms, chopped onion, eggplant, or finely minced vegetables, cut the meat into smaller pieces. Food will be able to cook at the same rate thanks to this.

• Meats with less fat and connective tissue, such as beef chuck or pig shoulder, will cook more quickly than lean meats like chicken or pork tenderloin.

• The meat needs to be placed such that it lies inside the stoneware and is not in contact with the lid.

• Cooking frozen meats (such as roasts or birds) requires adding at least 1 cup of heated liquid first. As a "cushion," the liquid will stop abrupt temperature swings. Meats should be cooked an extra 4 hours on LOW or 2 hours on HIGH in the majority of recipes that call for cubed frozen meat. Large frozen beef slices may require significantly more time to thaw and tenderize.

Fish

• Because fish cooks fast, it should be added after the cooking process, between the final fifteen and one

hours.
SPECIALTY Foods • To cook quickly and presentably, specialty dishes like stuffed chops or steak rolls, filled cabbage leaves, stuffed peppers, or baked apples can be stacked in a single layer.

Cleaning

Let the device cool after unplugging it from the wall socket.

NEVER let any liquid, including water, touch the main housing.

Wipe a moist towel over the main housing and the control panel to clean them.

Warm, soapy water should be used to wash the cooking pot, steaming/roasting rack, and glass cover.

Dishwasher cleaning is possible for the cooking pot, steaming/roasting rack, and glass lid.

Every time you use a part, dry it.

Fill the cooking pot with water and let it soak before cleaning if food residue has trapped on it. AVOID using scouring pads. Use a non-abrasive cleaner or liquid detergent with a nylon pad or brush if scouring is required.

Cooking Tips and Warnings

Always fill the stoneware ½ to ¾ full to adhere to stated cook times to prevent over- or under-cooking.

Sparingly fill stoneware. Never fill stoneware more than ¾ full to avoid spills.

Always cook for the prescribed amount of time with the lid on.

During the first two hours of cooking, do not remove the lid.

Wear oven gloves whenever you handle the lid or any stoneware.

After cooking and before cleaning, unplug all electronics.

To avoid overcooking and overflow, always fill your slow cooker to about three-quarters of the way.

Never peek! Heat is released when the lid is opened to check on your meal, which increases cooking time.

Yes, practically any recipe can be converted into a slow cooker dinner. Use these instructions or locate a similar recipe that has been written as a slow cooker recipe.

The finest companion for a meal planner is a slow cooker. One-pot slow cooker recipes make sure you're not left with a lot of dirty dishes, and freezer-friendly slow cooker dinners ensure you can always have supper on hand.

When used, this gadget produces heat. Avoid touching warm surfaces. Use knobs or handles.

Avoid submerging cords, plugs, or appliances in water or other liquids to prevent electric shock.

Children or those with impaired physical, sensory, or mental skills should not use this equipment.

Any appliance used near youngsters must be closely supervised. The device shouldn't be used by kids as playthings.

When not in use, before putting on or taking off parts, and before cleaning, unplug from the outlet. Before putting components on or taking them off, as well as before cleaning, let them cool. Turn off any controls before unplugging the power wire from the socket to detach it. Never cut the power by tugging on the cable.

Never use an appliance that has a broken cable or plug, isn't working properly, or has otherwise sustained harm. Never try to repair or splice a broken cord. Send the appliance back to the maker for inspection, maintenance, or adjusting (see warranty).

Injury may result from using accessory attachments that the appliance manufacturer does not suggest.

Use only indoors; never outside or for profit.

Do not allow the cord to touch hot surfaces or dangle over the edge of a table or counter.

Placement on or near moist surfaces, near heat sources like hot gas or electric burners, or inside a heated oven is not recommended.

When transferring an appliance that contains hot oil or other hot liquids, extreme caution must be utilized.

The remaining heat from the cooking cycle is applied to the heating base. Avoid touching the heating base right away after removing the stoneware. Before handling it, let it cool.

When opening the lid during or following a cooking cycle, exercise care. Burns can occur when steam escapes.

Use the equipment just for what it was designed for. Injuries may result from misuse.

Only for use on domestic countertops. Keep your distance from the wall and all sides at least 6 inches (152 mm). Always operate the equipment on a flat, dry surface.

A hot pot should not be filled with chilled food or cold drinks to prevent rapid temperature fluctuations.

Tempered glass is used to make the slow cooker cover. Always look for cracks, chips, or other damage on the lid. If the glass cover is broken, don't use it since it can break while you're using it.

Frequently Asked Questions

1. What distinguishes a slow cooker from a crock pot?

There is no distinction. The name brand "Crock-Pot" is referred to generally as a "slow cooker."

2. What is the difference between my crock-LOW pots and HIGH settings?

It only depends on how long it takes to get to the simmer point because HIGH and LOW are stable at the same temperature. The amount of time needed to cook food to the point where taste and texture are at their best depends on the cut and weight of the meat after it reaches the simmering phase. (You can cook most meals on either HIGH or LOW.

3. Can HIGH and LOW cook times be converted?

You can, indeed. 3 hours High to 7 hours Low. 4 hours High to 8 hours Low. 5 hours High to 9 hours Low. 6 hours High to 10 hours Low.

4. How full should my slow cooker be?

For optimal results, a slow cooker should be at least half filled.

5. Does water in a slow cooker evaporate?

Evaporation occurs relatively seldom in slow cookers. Remember that your finished result may be thicker when converting a recipe intended for the stovetop; additional water added throughout or after cooking will help thin it down.

6. Do I need to stir while my Crock-Pot cooks?

You don't need to stir during cooking for the majority of recipes. When you open the lid to stir, the heat within your slow cooker diminishes, lengthening the cooking time.

7. Is it okay to let my slow cooker simmer while I'm away from home?

You can, indeed. Place your slow cooker on a spotless, level surface to make sure it is secure when cooking unattended. To prevent the cable from angling off the counter, make sure nothing is touching your crock-pot and tuck it up and out of the way. It could be a good idea to prevent your pets from entering the kitchen if you have curious animals that might be enticed to check what is cooking while you are away.

8. How can I avoid over- or undercooking food?

Except for some cakes and custards, always fill the stoneware halfway to three-quarters of the way full to adhere to suggested cook times. Additionally, if a recipe specifies a range of cooking times, cook for the shortest time possible, check your meal, and then cook longer if necessary.

9. Can I use baking bags or aluminum foil in my crock pot?

Yes, you can!

10. How can I prevent my food in the slow cooker from becoming mushy?

To prevent your food from becoming excessively wet in your slow cooker, here are a few tips and tactics. One of the easiest methods is to routinely check on what's cooking, either with a glance or a more precise temperature reading.

11. What is the duration of the Keep Warm setting?

4 hours (standard)

12. Are BPA-free slow cooker liners available?

By US FDA 21CFR, 177.1500 - Nylon resins for cooking temperatures up to 400°F - the Crockpot Slow Cooker Liners are BPA-free.

4-Week Meal Plan

Week 1

Day 1:
Breakfast: Delicious Cheese Ham Omelet
Lunch: Maple-Pecan Brussels
Dinner: Chicken & Pineapple in Barbecue Sauce
Dessert: Tangy Chocolate Fondue

Day 2:
Breakfast: Bacon Strata
Lunch: Tasty Sweet Potatoes
Dinner: Cheese Beef Sandwiches
Dessert: Classical Cherry Chocolate Cake

Day 3:
Breakfast: Healthy Blueberry-Coconut Quinoa
Lunch: Loaded Baked Potatoes with Avocado
Dinner: Refreshing Salsa Verde Chicken
Dessert: Baked Apples

Day 4:
Breakfast: Apple Oatmeal
Lunch: Cauliflower-Pecan Casserole with Eggs
Dinner: Creamy Swiss Steak
Dessert: Warm Vanilla Pear Crisp

Day 5:
Breakfast: Creamy Blueberry-Banana Oatmeal
Lunch: Kale & Bacon Stew
Dinner: Caribbean-style Chicken Curry
Dessert: Traditional Blackberry Cobbler

Day 6:
Breakfast: Banana French Toast
Lunch: Pumpkin and Yogurt Soup
Dinner: Flank Steak Tacos
Dessert: Vibrant Blueberry Crisp

Day 7:
Breakfast: Easy Breakfast Barley
Lunch: Garlicky Button Mushrooms
Dinner: Gingered Chicken Thighs
Dessert: Pound Cake

Week 2

Day 1:
Breakfast: Soft Buttery Coconut Bread
Lunch: Tofu and Mushroom Curry with Nuts
Dinner: Delicious Cheese Stuffed Meatballs
Dessert: Lemon Cake

Day 2:
Breakfast: Herbed Meatloaf
Lunch: Thai-Style Green Curry with Tofu & Vegetables
Dinner: Coconut Chicken Stew
Dessert: Ginger Cake With Whipped Cream

Day 3:
Breakfast: Delicious Huevos Rancheros
Lunch: Green Beans & Mushroom Casserole
Dinner: Asian-Style Orange Chicken
Dessert: Creamy Chocolate Nut Cheesecake

Day 4:
Breakfast: Mediterranean-Style Eggs
Lunch: Cheese Brown Rice and Vegetable Casserole
Dinner: Tropical Lemongrass Pork
Dessert: Classical Vanilla Cheesecake

Day 5:
Breakfast: Cauliflower–Hash Brown Bake
Lunch: Beet Salad with Blue Cheese & Nuts
Dinner: Healthy Kung Pao Chicken
Dessert: Classical Chocolate Cake

Day 6:
Breakfast: Smoked Salmon & Asparagus Quiche
Lunch: Mushroom Burritos
Dinner: Tangy Mustard-Herb Pork Chops
Dessert: Carrot Cake

Day 7:
Breakfast: Quinoa with Walnuts and Apples
Lunch: Mexican-style Lasagna
Dinner: Creamy Lime Beef
Dessert: Green Tea Pudding

Week 3

Day 1:
Breakfast: Pecan Barley Porridge with Blueberries
Lunch: Cheese Potato Lasagna
Dinner: Spicy Beef Short Ribs
Dessert: Sweet Lentil with Coconut

Day 2:
Breakfast: Overnight Oatmeal with Raisins
Lunch: Tuna and Mushroom Noodles
Dinner: Chicken Meatballs with Tropical Sauce
Dessert: Dates Pudding

Day 3:
Breakfast: Creamy Banana Walnut Bread
Lunch: Cheesy Lentil and Vegetable Stew
Dinner: Tangy Balsamic Roast Beef
Dessert: Chocolaty Crème Brûlée

Day 4:
Breakfast: Asparagus and Cauliflower Quiche
Lunch: Cheesy Cauliflower
Dinner: Spiced Chicken
Dessert: Crunchy Apple Brown Betty

Day 5:
Breakfast: Broccoli and Bacon Quiche
Lunch: Balsamic Bacon Vegetable Medley
Dinner: Spicy Beef Goulash
Dessert: Blueberry Muffin

Day 6:
Breakfast: Coconut Berries Granola
Lunch: Lemon Garlicky Asparagus
Dinner: Creamy Pork & Sausage Meatballs
Dessert: Homemade Pecan Cookie

Day 7:
Breakfast: Sausage Egg Scramble
Lunch: Buttery Cheese Brussels Sprouts
Dinner: Coconut Lime Chicken with Sweet Potatoes
Dessert: Pumpkin Pie

Week 4

Day 1:
Breakfast: Delicious Cheese Ham Omelet
Lunch: Cauliflower Risotto
Dinner: Pork Loin with Creamy Gravy
Dessert: Delicious Strawberry Ricotta Cheesecake

Day 2:
Breakfast: Bacon Strata
Lunch: Beans and Jasmine Rice with Veggie
Dinner: Sweet Chicken and Broccoli
Dessert: Creamy Custard

Day 3:
Breakfast: Healthy Blueberry-Coconut Quinoa
Lunch: Herbed Lentils
Dinner: Hot Beef Bourguignon
Dessert: Tangy Chocolate Fondue

Day 4:
Breakfast: Apple Oatmeal
Lunch: Sweet & Spicy Pinto Beans
Dinner: Chocolaty Chicken Stew
Dessert: Classical Cherry Chocolate Cake

Day 5:
Breakfast: Creamy Blueberry-Banana Oatmeal
Lunch: Cheesy Mushroom Risotto
Dinner: Swiss Steak and Carrot Stew
Dessert: Baked Apples

Day 6:
Breakfast: Banana French Toast
Lunch: Quinoa and Vegetables Casserole
Dinner: Tangy Beef and Olive
Dessert: Warm Vanilla Pear Crisp

Day 7:
Breakfast: Easy Breakfast Barley
Lunch: Tangy Barley and Mushroom
Dinner: One-Pot Whole Chicken with Thyme
Dessert: Traditional Blackberry Cobbler

Chapter 1 Breakfast

Delicious Cheese Ham Omelet

Prep time: 15 minutes | Cook time: 4 to 6 hours | Serves: 3

Cooking spray

6 eggs

1 tablespoon unsweetened almond milk

1 garlic clove, minced

½ teaspoon salt

¼ teaspoon freshly ground black pepper

200g ham, diced

2 red or green peppers, seeded and diced

1 small onion, diced

60g diced tomatoes

200g grated low-fat Cheddar cheese, divided

1. Grease the slow cooker with cooking spray. 2. In a bowl, whisk the eggs, almond milk, garlic, salt, and pepper. 3. Fold in the ham, peppers, onion, tomatoes, and 100g of grated cheese. 4. Pour the egg mixture into the slow cooker. 5. Cover the slow cooker and cook on low temp setting for 4 to 6 hours until the eggs are set. 6. Sprinkle with the remaining 100g of grated cheese before serving.

Per Serving: Calories 613; Fat 49.9g; Sodium 1447mg; Carbs 9.9g; Fibre 4g; Sugar 1.6g; Protein 22.9g

Bacon Strata

Prep time: 15 minutes | Cook time: 4 hours | Serves: 6

Nonstick cooking spray

135g French bread cubes, toasted

150g grated sharp Cheddar cheese

5 slices cooked bacon, crumbled

6 eggs

720ml milk

¾ teaspoon salt

¼ teaspoon freshly ground black pepper

1. Spray the slow cooker with cooking spray. Add the bread cubes, cheese, and bacon and stir to combine. 2. In a bowl, whisk the eggs, milk, salt, and pepper. Pour over the bread mixture. 3. Cover the slow cooker and cook on low temp setting for 4 hours. 4. Let it sit for 15 minutes before serving.

Per Serving: Calories 273; Fat 26.3g; Sodium 38mg; Carbs 17.4g; Fibre 9g; Sugar 7.8g; Protein 4.6g

Healthy Blueberry-Coconut Quinoa

Prep time: 10 minutes | Cook time: 3 hours | Serves: 4

125g quinoa, rinsed and drained

25g grated unsweetened coconut

1 tablespoon honey

1 (335g) can coconut milk

375g fresh blueberries

1. Put the quinoa in the slow cooker. Sprinkle the coconut over the top and then drizzle with the honey. 2. Stir coconut milk until smooth and even in consistency. Pour over the quinoa. 3. Cover the slow cooker and cook on low temp setting for 3 hours. 4. Stir the quinoa, then scoop it into four serving bowls. Top each bowl with blueberries and serve.

Per Serving: Calories 426; Fat 32.6g; Sodium 652mg; Carbs 5.2g; Fibre 2.3g; Sugar 1.7g; Protein 19.8g

Banana French Toast

Prep time: 10 minutes | Cook time: 4 to 5 hours | Serves: 6

Nonstick cooking spray

12 (2.5cm) slices whole-wheat baguette

4 eggs

180ml low-fat or fat-free milk, or unsweetened almond milk

1 tablespoon brown sugar

1 tablespoon vanilla extract

1 teaspoon ground cinnamon

2 ripe bananas, sliced

Juice of ½ lemon

2 tablespoons dairy-free or trans-fat–free soft margarine or coconut oil, melted

60g chopped walnuts or nut of choice

1. Spray the slow cooker with the cooking spray. Arrange the baguette slices on the bottom of the slow cooker. 2. Whisk the eggs, milk, sugar, vanilla, and cinnamon. Pour over the baguette slices, making sure to cover each slice completely with the egg mixture. 3. In a mixing bowl, cover the banana slices with the lemon juice, tossing to coat. Place the banana slices atop the baguettes in the slow cooker. Drizzle with the melted margarine and sprinkle with the walnuts. Cover the slow cooker and cook on low temp setting for 4 to 5 hours until cooked through. 4. Serve warm.

Per Serving: Calories 216; Fat 11g; Sodium 523mg; Carbs 16g; Fibre 4g; Sugar 8g; Protein 7g

Apple Oatmeal

Prep time: 10 minutes | Cook time: 4 hours | Serves: 4

80g steel-cut oats

1 tablespoon unsalted butter, melted

960ml water

55g brown sugar

1 teaspoon ground cinnamon

½ teaspoon salt

1 Granny Smith apple, peeled, cored, and chopped

120ml milk

1. Combine the oats and butter in the slow cooker. Stir until the oats are coated with the butter. Add the water, brown sugar, cinnamon, and salt. 2. Cover the slow cooker and cook on low temp setting for 4 hours. 3. Stir the apple into the oatmeal. Scoop into four serving bowls and serve with a splash of milk.

Per Serving: Calories 412; Fat 33g; Sodium 623mg; Carbs 10g; Fibre 5g; Sugar 4g; Protein 21g

Creamy Blueberry-Banana Oatmeal

Prep time: 5 minutes | Cook time: 7 to 8 hours | Serves: 8

Nonstick cooking spray

160g steel-cut oats

1.4 L water

480ml low-fat or fat-free milk, or plant-based milk

375g fresh or frozen blueberries

1 ripe banana, mashed

1 teaspoon vanilla extract

2 teaspoons ground cinnamon

2 tablespoons brown sugar

Pinch salt

60g chopped walnuts, for garnish

1. Spray the slow cooker with the cooking spray. 2. Place the oats, water, milk, blueberries, banana, vanilla, cinnamon, brown sugar, and salt in the slow cooker. Stir well. Cover the slow cooker and cook on low temp setting for 7 to 8 hours. 3. Serve warm garnished with the chopped walnuts.

Per Serving: Calories 510; Fat 48g; Sodium 742mg; Carbs 17g; Fibre 9g; Sugar 6g; Protein 10g

Easy Breakfast Barley

Prep time: 5 minutes | Cook time: 7 to 8 hours | Serves: 6

1.7L water

370g hulled barley, rinsed well

1. Put the water and the barley in a slow cooker. Stir well. Cover the slow cooker and cook on low temp setting for 7 to 8 hours. 2. Serve warm with toppings such as fresh fruit, cinnamon, a dash vanilla extract, low-fat or plant-based milk, or chopped nuts.

Per Serving: Calories 201; Fat 10g; Sodium 542mg; Carbs 20g; Fibre 8g; Sugar 4g; Protein 8g

Soft Buttery Coconut Bread

Prep time: 10 minutes | Cook time: 3 to 4 hours | Serves: 4

1 tablespoon butter, softened

6 eggs

120ml coconut oil, melted

1 teaspoon pure vanilla extract

¼ teaspoon liquid stevia

100g almond flour

55g coconut flour

25g protein powder

1 teaspoon baking powder

1. Grease an 20-by-10cm loaf pan with the butter. 2. In a bowl, whisk the eggs, oil, vanilla, and stevia until well blended. 3. In a bowl, stir the almond flour, coconut flour, protein powder, and baking powder until mixed. 4. Add the dry ingredients to the wet ingredients and stir to combine. 5. Spoon the batter into the loaf pan and place the loaf pan on a rack in the slow cooker. 6. Cover the slow cooker and cook on low temp setting for 3 to 4 hours. 7. Cool the bread in the loaf pan for 15 minutes. then remove the bread from the pan and place onto a wire rack to cool completely.

Per Serving: Calories 265; Fat 17g; Sodium 633mg; Carbs 18g; Fibre 4g; Sugar 8g; Protein 8g

Herbed Meatloaf

Prep time: 10 minutes | Cook time: 3 hours | Serves: 8

1 tablespoon extra-virgin olive oil

900g pork mince

2 eggs

1 sweet onion, chopped

50g almond flour

2 teaspoons minced garlic

2 teaspoons dried oregano

1 teaspoon dried thyme

1 teaspoon fennel seeds

1 teaspoon freshly ground black pepper

½ teaspoon salt

1. Grease the slow cooker with the olive oil. 2. In a bowl, stir the pork, eggs, onion, almond flour, garlic, oregano, thyme, fennel seeds, pepper, and salt until well mixed. 3. Transfer the meat to the slow cooker's and shape it into a loaf, leaving about 1cm between the sides and meat. 4. Cover, and if slow cooker has a temperature probe, insert it. 5. Cook on low temp setting about 3 hours. 6. Slice in any way you prefer and serve.

Per Serving: Calories 353; Fat 28g; Sodium 521mg; Carbs 12g; Fibre 4g; Sugar 4g; Protein 11g

Delicious Huevos Rancheros

Prep time: 10 minutes | Cook time: 3 hours | Serves: 8

1 tablespoon extra-virgin olive oil

10 eggs

240g double cream

100g grated Monterey jack cheese, divided

265g prepared or homemade salsa

1 spring onion, green and white parts, chopped

1 jalapeño pepper, chopped

½ teaspoon chili powder

½ teaspoon salt

1 avocado, chopped, for garnish

1 tablespoon chopped coriander, for garnish

1. Lightly grease the slow cooker with the olive oil. 2. In a bowl, whisk the eggs, double cream, 50g of the cheese, salsa, spring onion, jalapeño, chili powder, and salt. pour the mixture into the cooker and sprinkle the top with the remaining cheese. 3. Cover and cook on low temp setting until the eggs are firm, about 3 hours on low temp setting. 4. Let the eggs cool slightly, then cut into wedges and serve garnished with avocado and coriander.

Per Serving: Calories 185; Fat 14g; Sodium 666mg; Carbs 10g; Fibre 3g; Sugar 4g; Protein 9g

Mediterranean-Style Eggs

Prep time: 10 minutes | Cook time: 5 to 6 hours | Serves: 4

1 tablespoon extra-virgin olive oil

12 eggs

120ml coconut milk

½ teaspoon dried oregano

½ teaspoon freshly ground black pepper

¼ teaspoon salt

60g chopped spinach

1 tomato, chopped

30g chopped sweet onion

1 teaspoon minced garlic

55g crumbled goat cheese

1. Grease the slow cooker with the olive oil. 2. In a bowl, whisk the eggs, coconut milk, oregano, pepper, and salt, until well blended. 3. Add the spinach, tomato, onion, and garlic, and stir to combine. 4. Pour the egg mixture into the insert and top with the crumbled goat cheese. 5. Cover the slow cooker and cook on low temp setting for 5 to 6 hours, until it is set like a quiche. 6. Serve warm.

Per Serving: Calories 451; Fat 30g; Sodium 421mg; Carbs 22g; Fibre 12g; Sugar 10g; Protein 30g

Cauliflower-Hash Brown Bake

Prep time: 15 minutes | Cook time: 6 hours | Serves: 6

1 tablespoon unsalted butter, Ghee

12 eggs

120g double cream

1 teaspoon salt, plus more for seasoning

½ teaspoon freshly ground black pepper, plus more for Seasoning

½ teaspoon ground mustard

1 head cauliflower, grated or minced

1 onion, diced

240g cooked breakfast sausage, sliced

200g grated Cheddar cheese, divided

1. Coat the slow cooker with the butter. 2. In a bowl, beat the eggs, then whisk in double cream, salt, pepper, and the ground mustard. 3. Spread about one-third of the cauliflower in an even layer in the cooker. 4. Layer one-third of the onions over the cauliflower, then one-third of the sausage, and top with 50g of Cheddar cheese. Spice with salt and pepper. Repeat twice more with the remaining ingredients. 5. Pour the egg mixture evenly over the layered ingredients, then sprinkle the Cheddar cheese on top. Cover and cook for 6 hours on low temp setting. Serve hot.

Per Serving: Calories 326; Fat 20g; Sodium 35mg; Carbs 13g; Fibre 7g; Sugar 2g; Protein 30g

Smoked Salmon & Asparagus Quiche

Prep time: 15 minutes | Cook time: 6 hours | Serves: 6

1 tablespoon extra-virgin olive oil

6 eggs

240g double cream

2 teaspoons chopped fresh dill, plus for garnish

½ teaspoon salt

¼ teaspoon freshly ground black pepper

150g grated Havarti or Monterey Jack cheese

300g asparagus, trimmed and sliced

150g smoked salmon, flaked

1. Coat the slow cooker with the olive oil. 2. In a bowl, beat the eggs, then whisk in the double cream, dill, salt, and pepper. 3. Stir in the cheese and asparagus. 4. Fold in the salmon and then pour the mixture into the prepared cooker. Cover and cook for 6 hours on low temp setting. Serve warm, garnished with fresh dill.

Per Serving: Calories 145; Fat 14g; Sodium 25mg; Carbs 6g; Fibre 0g; Sugar 2g; Protein 21g

Quinoa with Walnuts and Apples

Prep time: 15 minutes | Cook time: 2 hours | Serves: 4

Nonstick spray

170g quinoa, rinsed well

60g dried apples, chopped

60g chopped walnuts

85g maple syrup

½ teaspoon cinnamon

¼ teaspoon nutmeg

¼ teaspoon salt

1 (300g) can evaporated milk

120ml water

1. Spray the slow cooker with spray. Pour the quinoa into the cooker and stir in the apples, walnuts, maple syrup, cinnamon, nutmeg, and salt. 2. Add the milk and water to saucepan. Place over heat and heat to a bare simmer. Stir into the quinoa mixture. 3. Cover and cook on high temp setting for 2 hours, then turn off. Let sit for about 5 minutes before serving.

Per Serving: Calories 468; Fat 40g; Sodium 12mg; Carbs 4g; Fibre 2g; Sugar 1g; Protein 25g

Pecan Barley Porridge with Blueberries

Prep time: 15 minutes | Cook time: 8 to 9 hours | Serves: 4

Nonstick spray

210g pearl barley, rinsed

60g chopped pecan pieces

480ml water

1 (300g) can evaporated milk

55g packed brown sugar

¼ teaspoon salt

300g fresh blueberries, rinsed

1.Spray the slow cooker with spray. Heat a medium-sized frying pan over heat, then add the barley and chopped pecan pieces. Stir constantly for 1–2 minutes until begins to toast and smell nutty. 2. Immediately remove from heat and place mixture in the prepared slow cooker. 3. Carefully pour in the water and milk. Stir in the brown sugar and salt. 4. Cover the slow cooker and cook on low temp setting for 8–9 hours. Serve topped with blueberries.

Per Serving: Calories 353; Fat 28g; Sodium 521mg; Carbs 12g; Fibre 4g; Sugar 4g; Protein 11g

Overnight Oatmeal with Raisins

Prep time: 15 minutes | Cook time: 8 to 9 hours | Serves: 6

Nonstick spray

160g old-fashioned rolled oats

2 (300g) cans evaporated milk

100g raisins

30g toasted walnut pieces

1 teaspoon cardamom

¼ teaspoon salt

1.Spray the slow cooker with spray. In a bowl, stir the oats, milk, raisins, walnut pieces, cardamom, and salt. Pour into the prepared cooker. 2. Cover the slow cooker and cook on low temp setting for 8–9 hours. Serve hot.

Per Serving: Calories 185; Fat 14g; Sodium 666mg; Carbs 10g; Fibre 3g; Sugar 4g; Protein 9g

Creamy Banana Walnut Bread

Prep time: 15 minutes | Cook time: 6 hours | Serves: 6

1 tablespoon unsalted butter

1 (455g) loaf bread, cut into 1.5 – 2cm cubes

1 (200g) package cream cheese

2 ripe bananas

120g walnuts, coarsely chopped

12 eggs

85g maple syrup

240g milk or double cream

¼ teaspoon salt

Additional maple syrup for serving

1. Coat the bottom and sides of slow cooker with the butter. Place a third of the bread cubes in the bottom of the cooker. 2. Cut the cream cheese into 1cm cubes and evenly spread half of them over the bread cubes. 3. Slice 1 of the bananas, arrange the slices over the cream cheese layer, and sprinkle half of the walnut pieces over the banana. 4. Add another 200g bread cubes and create cream cheese, banana, and walnut layer over the top of the bread. Add the remaining bread cubes to the cooker. Press the mixture down slightly. 5. Place the eggs in a bowl and whisk until frothy. Whisk in the syrup, milk or cream, and salt. Pour over the bread in the insert. Cover and refrigerate for 12 hours. 6. After 12 hours, remove the insert from the refrigerator and place in the slow cooker. Cover the slow cooker and cook on low temp setting for 6 hours. Serve with warm maple syrup if desired.

Per Serving: Calories 221; Fat 11g; Sodium 1021mg; Carbs 0g; Fibre 0g; Sugar 0g; Protein 30g

Asparagus and Cauliflower Quiche

Prep time: 10 minutes | Cook time: 6 to 8 hours | Serves: 8

Cooking spray

12 eggs

120ml low-fat skimmed milk

280g grated part-skim mozzarella cheese

1 teaspoon salt

¼ teaspoon freshly ground black pepper

1 medium head cauliflower, grated or riced

455g asparagus, chopped

1. Coat a slow cooker with cooking spray. 2. In a bowl, whisk the eggs, milk, cheese, salt, and pepper. 3. Add the cauliflower to the bottom of the slow cooker. Top with half the asparagus. Repeat with the remaining cauliflower and asparagus. 4. Pour the eggs into the slow cooker. 5. Cook on low temp setting for 6 to 8 hours until eggs are set.

Per Serving: Calories 326; Fat 20g; Sodium 35mg; Carbs 13g; Fibre 7g; Sugar 2g; Protein 30g

Broccoli and Bacon Quiche

Prep time: 5 minutes | Cook time: 6 to 8 hours | Serves: 8

Cooking spray

8 eggs

480ml low fat milk

50g grated Parmesan cheese

½ teaspoon salt

900g frozen broccoli florets, thawed

150g bacon, cooked and crumbled

75g grated medium Cheddar cheese, divided

1. Coat a slow cooker with cooking spray. 2. In a bowl, whisk the eggs, milk, Parmesan, and salt. 3. Add the broccoli, bacon, and half the Cheddar cheese to the slow cooker. Pour in the egg mixture. Top with the Cheddar cheese. 4. Cook on low temp setting for 6 to 8 hours until the eggs are set.

Per Serving: Calories 145; Fat 14g; Sodium 25mg; Carbs 6g; Fibre 0g; Sugar 2g; Protein 25g

Coconut Berries Granola

Prep time: 10 minutes | Cook time: 6 hours | Serves: 8

Cooking spray

300g almonds

25g unsweetened coconut flakes

60g dried berries

40g chia seeds

1 teaspoon cinnamon

½ teaspoon salt

¼ teaspoon nutmeg

60g coconut oil

1 teaspoon vanilla

1. Grease the sides of a slow cooker with cooking spray. 2. Add the almonds, coconut flakes, dried berries, chia seeds, cinnamon, salt, and nutmeg to the slow cooker. 3. In a bowl, melt the coconut oil. Whisk in the vanilla. 4. Pour the mixture into the slow cooker, stirring. 5. Lay a small towel in between the slow cooker and the lid to create a barrier. 6. Cook mixture on low for 6 hours. 7. Transfer the granola to a baking sheet to cool.

Per Serving: Calories 273; Fat 31g; Sodium 12mg; Carbs 0g; Fibre 0g; Sugar 0g; Protein 1g

Sausage Egg Scramble

Prep time: 5 minutes | Cook time: 6 hours | Serves: 8

Cooking spray

200g low-fat pork sausage meat

12 eggs

455g low-fat Cheddar cheese, grated

120ml almond milk

½ teaspoon salt

¼ teaspoon freshly ground black pepper

1. Coat a slow cooker with cooking spray. 2. Add sausage, eggs, cheese, almond milk, salt, and pepper to the slow cooker. Stir to mix well. 3. Cook on low temp setting for 6 to 8 hours until the eggs are set. 4. "scramble" the mixture before serving.

Per Serving: Calories 468; Fat 40g; Sodium 12mg; Carbs 4g; Fibre 2g; Sugar 1g; Protein 25g

Maple-Pecan Brussels

Prep time: 10 minutes | Cook time: 4 to 5 hours | Serves: 6

900g Brussels sprouts, halved

2 red onions, sliced

70g pure maple syrup

2 tablespoons apple cider vinegar

1 tablespoon extra-virgin olive oil

1 teaspoon ground cinnamon

60g chopped pecans

1. Put the Brussels sprouts and onions in a slow cooker. 2. In a bowl, stir the maple syrup, vinegar, cinnamon, and olive oil. Pour this mixture over the vegetables and toss to coat. 3. Cover the slow cooker and cook on low temp setting for 4 to 5 hours. The Brussels sprouts should be softened but not mushy. 4. Add the pecans and stir to combine.

Per Serving: Calories 319; Fat 26.2g; Sodium 463mg; Carbs 10.7g; Fibre 0.4g; Sugar 5.0g; Protein 7.9g

Tasty Sweet Potatoes

Prep time: 5 minutes | Cook time: 7 to 8 hours | Serves: 6

6 sweet potatoes, washed and dried

1. Loosely ball up 7 or 8 pieces of aluminum foil and place them in the bottom of a slow cooker. 2. Prick each sweet potato 6 to 8 times with a fork. Wrap each potato in a piece of foil and seal it completely. Place the wrapped sweet potatoes in the slow cooker on top of the balls of foil. 3. Cover the slow cooker and cook on low temp setting for 7 to 8 hours remove the sweet potatoes from the slow cooker. Allow the potatoes to cool slightly, then unwrap from the foil. Serve hot.

Per Serving: Calories 268; Fat 22.1g; Sodium 650mg; Carbs 1g; Fibre 0.1g; Sugar 0.5g; Protein 12.8g

Loaded Baked Potatoes with Avocado

Prep time: 10 minutes | Cook time: 7 to 8 hours | Serves: 8

8 Russet potatoes

Extra-virgin olive oil cooking spray

510g creamy queso dip

1 avocado, cubed

15g chopped chives

1. Lightly spray the potatoes all over with the olive oil cooking spray. Wrap them in aluminum foil and place in a slow cooker. Cover and cook for 7 to 8 hours. 2. Remove each potato, slice lengthwise, and fluff the inside with the tines of a fork. Add some of the queso dip, being careful to keep it inside the potato skins. 3. Rewrap the potatoes in the foil and return them to the slow cooker for 30 minutes more until the queso is warmed through. 4. Serve topped with the avocado cubes and chopped chives.

Per Serving: Calories 228; Fat 21.4g; Sodium 135mg; Carbs 1g; Fibre 0.3g; Sugar 0.2g; Protein 6.8g

Cauliflower-Pecan Casserole with Eggs

Prep time: 15 minutes | Cook time: 6 hours | Serves: 6

1 tablespoon extra-virgin olive oil

900g cauliflower florets

10 bacon slices, cooked and chopped

120g chopped pecans

4 garlic cloves, sliced

½ teaspoon salt

½ teaspoon freshly ground black pepper

2 tablespoons freshly squeezed lemon juice

4 hardboiled eggs, grated, for garnish

1 spring onion, white and green parts, chopped, for garnish

1. Lightly grease the slow cooker with the olive oil. 2. In a bowl, toss the cauliflower, bacon, pecans, garlic, salt, and pepper. 3. Transfer the mixture to the slow cooker and sprinkle the lemon juice over the top. 4. Cover the slow cooker and cook on low temp setting for 6 hours. 5. Garnish with hard-boiled eggs and spring onion and serve.

Per Serving: Calories 200; Fat 13.2g; Sodium 473mg; Carbs 13.4g; Fibre 5.5g; Sugar 1.6g; Protein 8.5g

Kale & Bacon Stew

Prep time: 15 minutes | Cook time: 6 hours | Serves: 8

2 tablespoons bacon fat

900g kale, rinsed and chopped roughly

12 bacon slices, cooked and chopped

2 teaspoons minced garlic

480ml vegetable stock

Salt, for Seasoning

Freshly ground black pepper, for Seasoning

1. Grease the slow cooker with the bacon fat. 2. Add the kale, bacon, garlic, and stock to the insert. Gently toss to mix. 3. Cover the slow cooker and cook on low temp setting for 6 hours. 4. Spice with salt and pepper, and serve hot.

Per Serving: Calories 354; Fat 8.2g; Sodium 614mg; Carbs 8.1g; Fibre 0.6g; Sugar 6.7g; Protein 8.2g

Pumpkin and Yogurt Soup

Prep time: 15 minutes | Cook time: 7 to 8 hours | Serves: 6

3 tablespoons extra-virgin olive oil, divided

455g pumpkin, cut into 2.5cm chunks

120ml coconut milk

1 tablespoon apple cider vinegar

½ teaspoon chopped thyme

1 teaspoon chopped oregano

¼ teaspoon salt

240g Greek yogurt

1. Lightly grease the slow cooker with 1 tablespoon of the olive oil. 2. Add the remaining 2 tablespoons of the olive oil with the pumpkin, coconut milk, apple cider vinegar, thyme, oregano, and salt to the insert. 3. Cover the slow cooker and cook on low temp setting for 7 to 8 hours. 4. Using a masher to mash the pumpkin with the yogurt until smooth. 5. Serve warm.

Per Serving: Calories 274; Fat 23.9g; Sodium 80mg; Carbs 18.5g; Fibre 3.4g; Sugar 1.3g; Protein 6.4g

Garlicky Button Mushrooms

Prep time: 10 minutes | Cook time: 6 hours | Serves: 8

3 tablespoons extra-virgin olive oil

455g button mushrooms, wiped clean and halved

2 teaspoons minced garlic

¼ teaspoon salt

⅛ teaspoon freshly ground black pepper

2 tablespoons chopped fresh parsley

1. Place the olive oil, mushrooms, garlic, salt, and pepper in the slow cooker and toss to coat. 2. Cover the slow cooker and cook on low temp setting for 6 hours. 3. Serve tossed with the parsley.

Per Serving: Calories 229; Fat 28g; Sodium 172mg; Carbs 7g; Fibre 4g; Sugar 1g; Protein 8g

Tofu and Mushroom Curry with Nuts

Prep time: 15 minutes | Cook time: 6 hours | Serves: 4

2 tablespoons coconut oil, melted

675g extra-firm tofu, cut into 2.5cm cubes

300g cremini or button mushrooms, halved or litreered

55g diced onion

2 garlic cloves, minced

1 tablespoon grated fresh ginger

3 tablespoons curry powder

1 teaspoon ground cumin

1 teaspoon salt

½ teaspoon cayenne pepper

1 (350g) can coconut milk

40g chopped macadamia nuts

10g chopped fresh coriander

1. Grease the slow cooker with the coconut oil. Add the tofu, mushrooms, onion, garlic, ginger, curry powder, cumin, salt, cayenne, and coconut milk. Cover and cook for 6 hours on low temp setting. 2. Serve hot, garnished with the macadamia nuts and coriander.

Per Serving: Calories 199; Fat 16g; Sodium 313mg; Carbs 9g; Fibre 6g; Sugar 1g; Protein 8g

Thai-Style Green Curry with Tofu & Vegetables

Prep time: 15 minutes | Cook time: 7 hours | Serves: 4

2 tablespoons coconut oil

½ onion, diced

1 tablespoon minced fresh ginger

2 garlic cloves, minced

455g firm tofu, diced

½ green pepper, seeded and sliced

1 (350g) can coconut milk

65g Thai green curry paste

1 tablespoon erythritol

1 teaspoon salt

½ teaspoon turmeric

10g chopped fresh coriander, for garnish

1. In a frying pan, heat the coconut oil over medium-high heat. 2. Add the onion and sauté until softened, about 5 minutes. 3. Stir in the ginger and garlic. Transfer the mixture to the slow cooker. 4. Mix it with tofu, green pepper, coconut milk, curry paste, erythritol, salt, and turmeric. 5. Cover and cook for 7 hours on low temp setting. Serve hot, garnished with the coriander.

Per Serving: Calories 200; Fat 18g; Sodium 178mg; Carbs 4g; Fibre 2g; Sugar 1g; Protein 7g

Green Beans & Mushroom Casserole

Prep time: 15 minutes | Cook time: 6 hours | Serves: 4

1 tablespoon coconut oil

½ onion, diced

150g cremini or button mushrooms, sliced

2 garlic cloves, minced

2 teaspoons paprika

½ teaspoon salt

¼ teaspoon freshly ground black pepper

120ml Vegetable Stock(here)

455g firm tofu, cut into 2.5cm cubes

100g chopped green beans

1 (350g) can coconut milk

60g sliced almonds

1. In a frying pan, heat the coconut oil over medium-high heat. 2. Add the onion and sauté until it begins to soften, about 3 minutes. 3. Add the mushrooms and sauté until softened, about 5 minutes. 4. Stir in the garlic and sauté for about 30 seconds. 5. Stir in the paprika, salt, and pepper, and then add the vegetable stock to deglaze the frying pan, scraping up any browned bits from the bottom. Transfer to the slow cooker. 6. Stir the tofu, green beans, and coconut milk into the cooker. Cover and cook for 6 hours on low temp setting. Serve hot, garnished with the almonds.

Per Serving: Calories 194; Fat 17g; Sodium 243mg; Carbs 6g; Fibre 3g; Sugar 1g; Protein 7g

Cheese Brown Rice and Vegetable Casserole

Prep time: 15 minutes | Cook time: 3 to 4 hours | Serves: 8

1½ tablespoons olive oil, divided

2 medium onions, chopped

1 (250g) package sliced mushrooms

2 red peppers, chopped

1 jalapeño pepper, minced

800g cooked brown rice

360ml milk

2 eggs

120g low-fat sour cream

120g grated mozzarella cheese

50g grated Cheddar or Colby cheese

1. Grease a 4 or 6 litre slow cooker with olive oil and set aside. Heat remaining olive oil in a saucepan over medium-high heat. When hot, add the onions and mushrooms and cook, stirring occasionally, for 3 minutes. 2. Add the peppers and jalapeño and cook for 3–4 minutes longer until vegetables are crisp-tender. 3. In a bowl, combine the rice, milk, eggs, sour cream, mozzarella cheese, and Cheddar cheese. Layer half of this mixture in the prepared cooker. 4. Top the rice mixture with the vegetables, then spread the remaining rice mixture over the top. 5. Cover and cook on high temp setting for 3–4 hours. Serve hot.

Per Serving: Calories 317; Fat 26g; Sodium 407mg; Carbs 8g; Fibre 2g; Sugar 2g; Protein 16g

Beet Salad with Blue Cheese & Nuts

Prep time: 15 minutes | Cook time: 3 to 4 hours | Serves: 8

6 medium beetroot (about 2 bunches), cleaned and trimmed

4 tablespoons olive oil, divided

240g spring or baby salad greens

60ml balsamic vinegar

½ teaspoon salt

¼ teaspoon coarsely ground black pepper

60g crumbled blue cheese

40g toasted walnut pieces

1. Place the beetroot in a slow cooker. Toss with 2 tablespoons of oil. Cover and cook on high temp setting for 3–4 hours or until beetroot are easily pierced with a fork. 2. Place the hot beetroot on a chopping board. Let cool enough to handle, then remove and discard skins. Slice each beet into 8 wedges. Divide salad greens among 8 plates. Evenly top with beet wedges. 3. In a bowl, whisk the remaining olive oil with the balsamic vinegar, salt, and pepper. Pour over the salad. Sprinkle evenly with the crumbled blue cheese and toasted walnuts before serving.

Per Serving: Calories 243; Fat 23g; Sodium 336mg; Carbs 5g; Fibre 1.9g; Sugar 1g; Protein 5.45g

Cheesy Cauliflower

Prep time: 10 minutes | Cook time: 4 to 6 hours | Serves: 6

Cooking spray

2 medium heads cauliflower, cut into small florets

1 small onion, diced

720g Cheese Sauce

1. Coat a slow cooker with cooking spray. 2. Add the cauliflower and onion to the slow cooker. 3. Pour the cheese sauce over the top. 4. Cook on low temp setting for 4 to 6 hours or on high for 2 to 3 hours until the cauliflower is tender.

Per Serving: Calories 143; Fat 11g; Sodium 289mg; Carbs 4g; Fibre 1g; Sugar 1g; Protein 9g

Mexican-style Lasagna

Prep time: 15 minutes | Cook time: 2 to 3 hours | Serves: 8

1 tablespoon olive oil

1 (375g) can fire-roasted diced tomatoes, drained

1 medium-sized onion, peeled and diced

4 cloves garlic, minced

1 tablespoon chili powder

2 teaspoons paprika, sweet or smoked

½ tablespoon ground cumin

1 (375g) can black beans, drained and rinsed

190g sliced black olives

400g cooked rice

1 (300 to 400g) jar roasted salsa verde

1 (12-count) package corn tortillas

2 (200g) packages grated Cheddar cheese

240g Enchilada Sauce

1 (300g) bag frozen corn, defrosted

15g chopped coriander leaves

120g sour cream

1. Heat oil in a frying pan over medium-high heat. Add the tomatoes, onion, and garlic, cook for 5 minutes until onions are softened. 2. Add the chili powder, paprika, and cumin. Stir for 1 minute. Stir in the black beans, olives, and cooked rice. 3. Spread half of the jar of salsa verde in the bottom of a slow cooker. Place 2 or 3 tortillas over the sauce. 4. Spread half of the rice mixture over the tortillas. Sprinkle half of the cheese over the rice. 5. Place another layer of tortillas on top of the cheese. Pour all of the enchilada sauce evenly over the tortillas. Pour all the corn evenly over the sauce, followed by the remaining rice mixture. 6. Add a final layer of tortillas over the rice mixture. Pour the remaining salsa verde evenly over the tortillas, using the spoon spread the sauce, followed by the remaining cheese. 7. Cover and cook on high temp setting for 2½–3 hours until the cheese has completely melted and the sauce is bubbling. 8. Sprinkle on the coriander and garnish with sour cream, if desired.

Per Serving: Calories 433; Fat 24g; Sodium 668mg; Carbs 12g; Fibre 4g; Sugar 3g; Protein 24g

Cheese Potato Lasagna

Prep time: 15 minutes | Cook time: 3 to 4 hours | Serves: 8

1 (375g) container ricotta cheese

100g grated Parmesan cheese

1 (400g) package grated mozzarella or Cheddar cheese

2 eggs, lightly beaten

¼ teaspoon ground black pepper

1 teaspoon dried basil

½ teaspoon dried oregano

960g Marinara Sauce, divided

6 Yukon gold potatoes, peeled and thinly sliced

1. In a bowl, combine the 3 cheeses, eggs, pepper, basil, and oregano. Set aside. 2. Spread about 80g of marinara sauce into the slow cooker to cover the bottom with a thin layer. Top with a third of the sliced potatoes. 3. Spread half of the cheese mixture on top of the potatoes. Spoon a third of the remaining sauce over the cheese. 4. Layer another third of the potatoes. 5. Top with the remaining cheese mixture and another layer of the sauce. 6. Layer the remaining potatoes over the sauce and top with remaining sauce, making sure that all the potatoes are coated. 7. Cover and cook on high temp setting for 3–4 hours until the potatoes are tender.

Per Serving: Calories 180; Fat 14g; Sodium 332mg; Carbs 5g; Fibre 2g; Sugar 1g; Protein 9g

Tuna and Mushroom Noodles

Prep time: 15 minutes | Cook time: 5 hours | Serves: 4

Cooking spray

1 (300g) package wide egg noodles

2 (125 – 150g) cans tuna packed in water, drained

1 (150g) can French fried onions divided

1 (350g) can cream of mushroom soup, undiluted

120ml evaporated milk

120ml vegetable stock

1 (100g) can sliced mushrooms, drained

1 (200g) package Cheddar cheese

50g grated Parmesan cheese

50g frozen peas, defrosted

1. Spray the slow cooker with the cooking spray. Add half of the egg noodles into the slow cooker. 2. Break up tuna in a bowl. Mix in half of the can of fried onions. Add tuna mixture on top of the noodles. Cover tuna with egg noodles. 3. Combine cream of mushroom soup, evaporated milk and vegetable stock; pour evenly over noodles. 4. Top with mushrooms and sprinkle evenly with the cheeses. 5. Top with remaining fried onions. Cook on low temp setting for 5 hours. Gently mix in the peas. 6. Cover the slow cooker and cook on low temp setting for 15 more minutes.

Per Serving: Calories 295; Fat 27g; Sodium 466mg; Carbs 7g; Fibre 3g; Sugar 1g; Protein 10g

Cheesy Lentil and Vegetable Stew

Prep time: 15 minutes | Cook time: 6 to 8 hours | Serves: 4

Nonstick cooking spray

1 tablespoon olive oil

3 medium carrots, peeled and diced

1 small onion, peeled and diced

180g fresh cauliflower florets, rinsed and coarsely chopped

1 sweet potato, peeled and cut into 2.5cm cubes

190g brown lentils, rinsed, drained, and inspected to remove any dirt or debris

½ teaspoon ground ginger

2 tablespoons soy sauce

¼ teaspoon black pepper

360ml Vegetable Stock

1 (125g) bag baby spinach leaves, rinsed and drained

50g grated Parmesan cheese

1. Spray a slow cooker with cooking spray. Heat the olive oil in a frying pan over medium-high heat. When hot, add the carrots and onion. Cook, for 5 minutes until the onions soften. 2. Add the cauliflower and sweet potatoes. Cook for 3–4 minutes longer, stirring frequently until vegetables are crisp-tender. 3. Add the sautéed vegetables to the slow cooker. Stir in the lentils, ginger, soy sauce, black pepper, and vegetable stock. Cover the slow cooker and cook on low temp setting for 6–8 hours. 4. Stir in the spinach, cover, and let sit for 15 minutes to allow spinach to wilt. 5. Ladle stew into bowls and sprinkle with Parmesan cheese just before serving.

Per Serving: Calories 242; Fat 19g; Sodium 241mg; Carbs 7g; Fibre 2g; Sugar 2g; Protein 13g

Cauliflower Risotto

Prep time: 15 minutes | Cook time: 4 to 5 hours | Serves: 4 to 6

455g riced cauliflower

1 celery stalk, minced

1 small shallot, minced

60ml vegetable stock

½ teaspoon garlic powder

½ teaspoon sea salt

Freshly ground black pepper

1. In slow cooker, combine the riced cauliflower, celery, shallot, stock, garlic powder, and salt, and spice with pepper. Stir well. 2. Cover the slow cooker and set to low temp setting. Cook for 4 to 5 hours and serve.

Per Serving: Calories 104; Fat 5.4g; Sodium 69mg; Carbs 25g; Fibre 5.4g; Sugar 9.8g; Protein 2.6g

Balsamic Bacon Vegetable Medley

Prep time: 15 minutes | Cook time: 4 to 6 hours | Serves: 4

Cooking spray

200g bacon, cooked and crumbled

1 small onion, chopped

2 peppers, seeded and chopped

75g carrots, peeled and chopped

75g green beans, cut into 2.5 cm pieces

75g Brussels sprouts, trimmed and halved

75g beetroot, peeled and chopped

75g courgette, chopped

60ml water

1 tablespoon extra-virgin olive oil

2 tablespoons balsamic vinegar

1. Coat a slow cooker with cooking spray. 2. Add the bacon, onion, peppers, carrots, green beans, Brussels sprouts, beetroot, and squash to the slow cooker. 3. In a bowl, mix the water, olive oil, and vinegar to make a sauce. Pour it over the top of the vegetables. 4. Cook on low temp setting for 4 to 6 hours or on high for 2 to 3 hours until Brussels sprouts are tender.

Per Serving: Calories 491; Fat 37g; Sodium 815mg; Carbs 13g; Fibre 4g; Sugar 3g; Protein 31g

Lemon Garlicky Asparagus

Prep time: 10 minutes | Cook time: 4 to 6 hours | Serves: 4

900g asparagus, ends trimmed

Juice of 2 lemons (4 to 6 tablespoons)

120ml low-sodium chicken stock or water

2 garlic cloves, minced

1 teaspoon basil

1 teaspoon garlic salt

½ teaspoon freshly ground black pepper

¼ teaspoon red pepper flakes

1 lemon, sliced

1. Place the asparagus in the slow cooker. 2. In a bowl, mix the lemon juice, stock, garlic, basil, garlic salt, black pepper, and red pepper flakes. 3. Pour the sauce over the asparagus, then top with the lemon slices. 4. Cook on low temp setting for 4 to 6 hours or on high for 2 to 3 hours.

Per Serving: Calories 280; Fat 25g; Sodium 289mg; Carbs 8g; Fibre 3g; Sugar 2g; Protein 11g

Mushroom Burritos

Prep time: 15 minutes | Cook time: 2 to 4 hours | Serves: 4

455g Portobello mushrooms, cleaned and sliced

2 garlic cloves, minced

1 tablespoon plus 1 teaspoon olive oil, divided

60g feta cheese, drained and crumbled

2 teaspoons balsamic vinegar

½ teaspoon salt

¼ teaspoon black pepper

1 teaspoon dried oregano

4 flour or whole wheat burrito-size tortillas

30g grated lettuce

2 Roma tomatoes, seeded and diced

240g tzatziki sauce

1. Mix the mushrooms, garlic, and 1 tablespoon of the olive oil in a slow cooker. Cover the slow cooker and cook on low temp setting for 2–4 hours. 2. Uncover the slow cooker and cook on low temp setting for another 30 minutes or until excess moisture evaporates. 3. Meanwhile, in a bowl, mix the cheese, remaining olive oil, balsamic vinegar, salt, black pepper, and oregano. Set aside, covered in the refrigerator. 4. Spoon the hot mushrooms evenly over the tortillas. Top with the cheese mixture. 5. Cover with the lettuce and tomatoes and top with tzatziki sauce, if desired. Roll up burrito-style and serve immediately.

Buttery Cheese Brussels Sprouts

Prep time: 15 minutes | Cook time: 6 to 8 hours | Serves: 8

Cooking spray

900g Brussels sprouts, trimmed and halved

55g butter, melted

2 tablespoons cornflour

30g chopped onion

240ml whole milk

200g grated Gruyère cheese

1. Coat a slow cooker with cooking spray. 2. Add the Brussels sprouts to the slow cooker. 3. In a bowl, mix the butter, cornflour, onion, whole milk, and cheese until well blended. Pour the mixture over the vegetables. 4. Cook on low temp setting for 6 to 8 hours or on high for 3 to 4 hours.

Per Serving: Calories 135; Fat 12g; Sodium 87mg; Carbs 12g; Fibre 3g; Sugar 1g; Protein 4g

Chapter 3 Beans and Grains

Beans and Jasmine Rice with Veggie

Prep time: 10 minutes | Cook time: 2 hours | Serves: 6

370g jasmine rice (dry white)

50g frozen peas

70g frozen carrots (diced)

70g frozen edamame beans

65g frozen, roasted corn

2 whisked eggs

1 teaspoon shallots, minced

2 tablespoon salted butter

1 teaspoon fresh ground pepper

2 teaspoons low sodium soy sauce

2 teaspoon Worcestershire sauce

1. Add 960ml water to a slow cooker. Add all stirred ingredients to the inner pot. 2. Close lid and let cook for 1½ to 2 hours on high temp setting.

Per Serving: Calories 158; Fat 10g; Sodium 332mg; Carbs 7.3g; Fibre 5.7g; Sugar 7.3g; Protein 3g

Baked Beans and Beef Stew

Prep time: 25 minutes | Cook time: 3 hours | Serves: 32

2 (700g) cans baked beans with pork

455g beef mince

455g bacon, cooked and crumbled

225g cooked ham, chopped

2 tablespoons minced onion

60g ketchup

1 tablespoon chili powder

55g packed brown sugar

1 tablespoon molasses

60ml water

120ml cooking oil

1. Using cooking oil preheat a frying pan. Crumble the beef mince in it over medium-high heat. Cook 5 to 10 minutes. 2. With the grease drained off transfer the beef to a slow cooker. Stir in the baked beans, bacon, ham, onion, chili powder, ketchup, brown sugar and molasses. 3. Cover and cook on high temp setting for 3 hours on low temp setting.

Per Serving: Calories 90; Fat 3.1g; Sodium 592mg; Carbs 10g; Fibre 4g; Sugar 0.8g; Protein 6.2g

Easy Dried Beans Stew

Prep time: 5 minutes | Cook time: 6 hours | Serves: 6

455g dried black beans, chickpeas, white beans, butter beans, navy beans, or pinto beans, picked over and rinsed

About 1.4L water or no-salt-added vegetable stock or chicken stock

1. In a slow cooker, combine the beans and water. 2. If the liquid doesn't cover the beans by about 8cm, add more. 3. Cover and cook on high temp setting for 4 to 6 hours, until the beans reach desired consistency. 4. Cool and store the beans in portions.

Per Serving: Calories 241; Fat 17.9g; Sodium 518mg; Carbs 8g; Fibre 3g; Sugar 3g; Protein 9.8g

Sweet & Spicy Pinto Beans

Prep time: 10 minutes | Cook time: 7 to 8 hours | Serves: 8

455g dried pinto beans, soaked overnight

1.2L beef stock

240g low-sodium tomato sauce

1 medium white onion, diced

1 jalapeño pepper, seeded, and finely diced

4 garlic cloves, minced

1 tablespoon ancho chili powder

1 teaspoon chili powder

1 teaspoon apple cider vinegar

1 teaspoon ground cumin

1 packed teaspoon brown sugar

1 teaspoon smoked paprika

½ teaspoon dried oregano

Freshly ground black pepper

1. Drain and rinse the soaked beans. Put them in a slow cooker along with the stock, tomato sauce, onion, jalapeño, garlic, ancho chili powder, chili powder, vinegar, cumin, sugar, paprika, and oregano. Cover the slow cooker and cook on low temp setting for 7 to 8 hours, until the beans are tender and the liquid has thickened slightly. 2. Taste and spice with the pepper. Serve warm.

Per Serving: Calories 490; Fat 39g; Sodium 896mg; Carbs 12g; Fibre 4g; Sugar 3g; Protein 28g

Lima Bean and Veggie Casserole

Prep time: 5 minutes | Cook time: 7 to 8 hours | Serves: 8

455g dried lima beans, soaked overnight

1 (200g) can no-salt-added tomatoes, diced

135g finely chopped sweet potato

1 medium carrot, finely chopped

1 onion, finely chopped

4 garlic cloves, minced

1 tablespoon dried mustard

½ teaspoon freshly ground black pepper

480ml water

1. Put the beans in a slow cooker along with the tomatoes, sweet potato, carrot, onion, garlic, dried mustard, pepper, and water. 2. Stir to combine. Cover the slow cooker and cook on low temp setting for 7 to 8 hours. 3. Serve warm.

Per Serving: Calories 275; Fat 23g; Sodium 629mg; Carbs 10g; Fibre 3.5g; Sugar 5.4g; Protein 4g

Sweet & Sour White Beans

Prep time: 5 minutes | Cook time: 7 to 8 hours | Serves: 8

455g white beans, soaked overnight

960ml Savoury Vegetable Stock

1 (150g) can no-salt-added tomato paste

240ml water

3 carrots, diced

1 sweet onion, diced

2 red, orange, yellow, or green peppers, diced

60g Homemade Ketchup

60ml dry cooking sherry

60ml low-sodium tamari

60ml cider vinegar

2 tablespoons sugar

1 tablespoon dried marjoram

1 tablespoon dried thyme

2 teaspoons freshly ground black pepper

1 tablespoon cornflour

1. Put beans in a slow cooker along with the stock, tomato paste, water, carrots, onion, peppers, ketchup, sherry, tamari, vinegar, sugar, marjoram, thyme, and pepper. Cover the slow cooker and cook on low temp setting for 7 to 8 hours. 2. With 15 minutes left before serving, stir in the cornflour . Cook for another 15 minutes until the stock thickens. 3. Serve warm.

Per Serving: Calories 140; Fat 7.9g; Sodium 1002mg; Carbs 6g; Fibre 2g; Sugar 2g; Protein 8g

Lime-Coconut Red Beans with Rice

Prep time: 5 minutes | Cook time: 7 to 8 hours | Serves: 8

185g dried red beans, soaked overnight

960ml Chicken Stock

1 (360g) can light coconut milk

300g long-grain basmati white rice

1 onion, finely diced

2 garlic cloves, minced

1 teaspoon red pepper flakes

½ teaspoon coconut extract

1 to 2 tablespoons freshly squeezed lime juice

2 limes, cut into wedges, for serving

1. Drain and rinse the soaked beans. Add the beans to a slow cooker along with the stock, coconut milk, rice, onion, garlic, red pepper flakes, and coconut extract. Stir well. Cover and cook for 7 to 8 hours on low temp setting. 2. Just before serving, stir in the lime juice and taste to adjust Seasonings. 3. Serve warm, with the lime wedges on the side.

Per Serving: Calories 215; Fat 16g; Sodium 1033mg; Carbs 10g; Fibre 4g; Sugar 3g; Protein 9g

Mushroom & Wild Rice Medley with Pecans

Prep time: 10 minutes | Cook time: 6 to 8 hours | Serves: 8

650g wild rice, rinsed and drained

1 tablespoon extra-virgin olive oil

1.4L Savoury Vegetable Stock

80g finely chopped shallots

200g sliced mushrooms

2 garlic cloves, minced

1 teaspoon dried thyme

Freshly ground black pepper

60g chopped pecans

1 tablespoon fresh rosemary

1. Add the wild rice and oil to a slow cooker and stir until the grains are well coated. Add the stock, shallots, mushrooms, garlic, thyme, and pepper and stir well. Cover the slow cooker and cook on low temp setting for 6 to 8 hours, until the rice is tender. 2. Stir in the pecans and fresh rosemary just before serving.

Per Serving: Calories 196; Fat 15g; Sodium 762mg; Carbs 11g; Fibre 5g; Sugar 2g; Protein 6g

Quinoa and Vegetables Casserole

Prep time: 10 minutes | Cook time: 6 to 7 hours | Serves: 8

340g quinoa, rinsed and drained

960ml savoury vegetable stock

1 medium onion, chopped

1 medium red pepper, chopped

2 medium carrots, chopped

100g fresh green beans, chopped

2 garlic cloves, minced

Freshly ground black pepper

1 teaspoon chopped fresh basil, for garnish

1. Put the quinoa, stock, onion, pepper, carrots, green beans, garlic, and pepper in a slow cooker. Stir to combine. Cover the slow cooker and cook on low temp setting for 6 to 7 hours, until the vegetables are tender and the liquid is absorbed into the quinoa. 2. Serve garnished with the fresh basil.

Per Serving: Calories 540; Fat 37g; Sodium 635mg; Carbs 16g; Fibre 8g; Sugar 2g; Protein 38g

Garlic Veggie with Lentils

Prep time: 15 minutes | Cook time: 7 to 8 hours | Serves: 8

575g dried lentils

1.2L savoury vegetable stock

1 (200g) can no-salt-added diced tomatoes

1 onion, chopped

2 leeks, chopped

8 garlic cloves, minced

2 carrots, chopped

2 bay leaves

1 teaspoon dried thyme

Freshly ground black pepper

1. Rinse lentils under cold water in a fine-mesh strainer. 2. Combine all of the ingredients in a slow cooker and stir. Cover the slow cooker and cook on low temp setting for 7 to 8 hours until the lentils are tender and the sauce has thickened. 3. Remove and discard the bay leaf. Serve warm.

Per Serving: Calories 282; Fat 23g; Sodium 242mg; Carbs 13g; Fibre 1g; Sugar 2g; Protein 9g

Cheesy Mushroom Risotto

Prep time: 15 minutes | Cook time: 1 to 2 hours | Serves: 6

1 teaspoon olive oil

55g finely diced onion

2 cloves garlic, minced

200g sliced mushrooms, any variety

480ml Vegetable Stock

385g Arborio rice

480ml water

120ml dry white wine

½ teaspoon salt

25g grated Parmesan cheese

1 tablespoon butter, softened

2 tablespoons minced parsley leaves

Additional 25g Parmesan cheese

1. Heat the oil in a pan. Sauté the onion, garlic, and mushrooms until soft, about 4–5 minutes. 2. Add stock and the rice and cook until the liquid is fully absorbed, about 5 minutes. 3. Transfer the rice mixture into a slow cooker. Sir in the water, wine, salt, and stock. Cover and cook on high temp setting for 1½–2 hours or until all the liquid has been absorbed. 4. Stir in Parmesan cheese and butter. Sprinkle with parsley and/or Parmesan cheese, if desired, before serving.

Per Serving: Calories 103; Fat 7g; Sodium 59mg; Carbs 13g; Fibre 2g; Sugar 1g; Protein 8g

Delicious Wild Mushroom Risotto

Prep time: 15 minutes | Cook time: 1 hours | Serves: 6

1 teaspoon olive oil

20g finely diced shallot

2 cloves garlic, minced

200g sliced assorted wild mushrooms

480ml Vegetable Stock

385g Arborio rice

720ml water

½ teaspoon salt

1. Heat the oil in a frying pan. Sauté the shallot, garlic, and mushrooms until soft, about 4–5 minutes. 2. Add 120ml stock and the rice and cook until the liquid is fully absorbed, about 5 minutes. 3. Scrape the rice mixture into a slow cooker. Add the water, salt, and remaining stock. 4. Cover the slow cooker and cook on low temp setting for 1 hour. Stir before serving.

Per Serving: Calories 217; Fat 18g; Sodium 71mg; Carbs 19g; Fibre 8g; Sugar 0g; Protein 8g

Beans in Barbecue Sauce

Prep time: 15 minutes | Cook time: 6 hours | Serves: 8

1 sweet onion, peeled and diced

3 (375g) cans cannellini, butter beans, or navy beans, drained and rinsed

240g barbecue sauce

160g molasses

1 teaspoon dry mustard powder

1 (35 – 50g) package beef jerky, finely chopped

Salt, to taste

1. Add all ingredients to a slow cooker. Stir until combined. Cover the slow cooker and cook on low temp for 6 hours. 2. Taste for seasoning and add salt, if needed.

Per Serving: Calories 260; Fat 21g; Sodium 71mg; Carbs 21g; Fibre 10g; Sugar 1g; Protein 11g

Cranberry Brown Bread

Prep time: 15 minutes | Cook time: 4 to 5 hours | Serves: 20

3 empty 400g cans

Nonstick cooking spray, as needed

Bamboo skewers, to fit slow cooker

60g rye flour

65g plain flour

65g polenta

1 tablespoon sugar

Water, as needed

½ teaspoon baking powder

½ teaspoon baking soda

½ teaspoon cinnamon

65g sweetened dried cranberries

½ teaspoon ground ginger

240ml buttermilk

105g molasses

1. Spray the insides of the 3 empty cans with cooking spray. Place a layer of bamboo skewers on the bottom of a slow cooker. 2. In a bowl, whisk the flours, polenta, sugar, baking powder, baking soda, cinnamon, cranberries, and ginger. Set the mixture aside. 3. In another bowl, stir the buttermilk and molasses. Pour into the dry mixture and stir until combined. Evenly divide the dough among the 3 cans. Cover each can with foil; stand the cans inside the slow cooker. 4. Add water until it is halfway up the sides of the cans. Cook on low temp setting for 4–5 hours or until a toothpick inserted into the bread comes out clean. Carefully remove the cans and allow them to cool for 5 minutes. 5. Then gently tap the cans and remove the bread. Allow the bread to cool on a wire rack. Slice them into 20 slices.

Per Serving: Calories 340; Fat 33g; Sodium 17mg; Carbs 7g; Fibre 3g; Sugar 3g; Protein 3g

Healthy Farro

Prep time: 5 minutes | Cook time: 2 hours | Serves: 4

255g farro, rinsed

960ml no-salt-added vegetable stock or chicken

stock or water

1 tablespoon extra-virgin olive oil

1. In a slow cooker, combine the farro, stock, and oil. 2. Cover and cook on high temp setting for 2 hours, until the farro is chewy but tender. 3. If the farro is done but there is still liquid in the pot, let it sit, uncovered, on the low temp setting for about 30 minutes, until the liquid is absorbed. 4. Serve immediately.

Per Serving: Calories 125; Fat 9.4g; Sodium 338mg; Carbs 7.8g; Fibre 3.0g; Sugar 3g; Protein 3.1g

Herbed Lentils

Prep time: 5 minutes | Cook time: 2 hours | Serves: 6

455g dried brown or green lentils, picked over and rinsed

1.4L no-salt-added vegetable stock or chicken stock

or water

1 bay leaf

Rosemary or thyme sprigs

1. In a slow cooker, combine the lentils, stock, bay leaf, and fresh herbs. If the liquid doesn't cover the lentils by about 5 cm, add more. 2. Cover and cook on high temp setting for 2 hours, until the lentils are done to your liking. 3. Serve. 4. Cool the lentils and store them in portions.

Per Serving: Calories 136; Fat 7.9g; Sodium 1013mg; Carbs 7.5g; Fibre 4g; Sugar 4g; Protein 6.3g

Tangy Barley and Mushroom

Prep time: 15 minutes | Cook time: 4 to 6 hours | Serves: 4

4 tablespoons olive oil, divided

185g uncooked barley

85g diced onion

1 (250g) package mushrooms, cleaned and sliced

1 teaspoon salt

¼ teaspoon pepper

2 (300g) cans beef stock, low-sodium preferred

15g chopped Italian flat-leafed parsley

1. Grease the slow cooker with ½ tablespoon of the olive oil. Heat 1 tablespoon olive oil over medium heat in a frying pan. When hot, add the barley and cook, stirring often, until it begins to smell toasty, about 2 minutes. 2. Transfer the barley to the slow cooker. Heat remaining oil in the same frying pan over medium-high heat. Add the onion and mushrooms. Sauté until the onions soften and begin to brown. 3. Add both vegetables to the cooker along with the salt, pepper, and beef stock. Cover the slow cooker and cook on low temp setting for 4–6 hours. 4. If there is too much liquid in the slow cooker, uncover and cook on high temp setting for an 30 minutes. Serve garnished with parsley.

Per Serving: Calories 173; Fat 13g; Sodium 394mg; Carbs 9g; Fibre 0g; Sugar 0g; Protein 12g

Chicken & Pineapple in Barbecue Sauce

Prep time: 5 minutes | Cook time: 6 hours | Serves: 6

900g boneless, skinless chicken thighs, trimmed of excess fat

1 red pepper, seeded and diced

1 (400g) bottle barbecue sauce

1 (200g) can crushed pineapple, drained of excess

juice

1 teaspoon garlic powder

Salt

Freshly ground black pepper

Steamed rice, for serving

1. Combine the chicken, pepper, barbecue sauce, crushed pineapple, and garlic powder in the slow cooker. Spice with salt and pepper and stir to combine. 2. Cover the slow cooker and cook on low temp setting for 6 hours until the chicken is tender. Season with salt and pepper. Serve the chicken and sauce over the rice.

Per Serving: Calories 410; Fat 30g; Sodium 963mg; Carbs 0g; Fibre 0g; Sugar 0g; Protein 35g

Lime Chicken with Guacamole Cream Sauce

Prep time: 5 minutes | Cook time: 6 hours | Serves: 4

900g boneless, skinless chicken thighs, trimmed of excess fat

285g salsa

1 teaspoon chili powder

1 teaspoon garlic powder

1 teaspoon ground cumin

2 tablespoons fresh lime juice

Salt

Freshly ground black pepper

60g guacamole

60g sour cream

1. Put the chicken in the slow cooker. Add the salsa, chili powder, garlic powder, and cumin. Stir to coat the chicken. 2. Cover the slow cooker and cook on low temp setting for 6 hours until the chicken is tender. 3. Transfer the chicken to a cutting board. Shred the chicken. Return the chicken to the slow cooker and stir in the lime juice. Spice with salt and pepper. 4. Serve the chicken topped with guacamole and sour cream.

Per Serving: Calories 650; Fat 54g; Sodium 863mg; Carbs 8g; Fibre 5g; Sugar 2g; Protein 33g

Refreshing Salsa Verde Chicken

Prep time: 10 minutes | Cook time: 5-6 hours | Serves: 6

Nonstick cooking spray

900g boneless, skinless chicken breasts

490g salsa verde

1 (360g) can no-salt-added fire-roasted tomatoes

1 (100g) can green chiles

1 pepper (any colour), chopped

2 teaspoons ground cumin

1 teaspoon dried oregano

Freshly ground black pepper

Optional toppings: chopped fresh coriander, avocado slices, lime wedges, lettuce leaves

1. Spray the slow cooker with the cooking spray. Place the chicken in the slow cooker. Add the salsa verde, tomatoes, chiles, pepper, cumin, oregano, and black pepper, and stir to combine. Cover the slow cooker and cook on low temp setting for 5 to 6 hours. 2. Remove the chicken and shred it. Stir the grated chicken back into the slow cooker and taste to adjust Seasonings. 3. Serve hot, with toppings such as chopped fresh coriander, avocado slices, or lime wedges, if desired.

Per Serving: Calories 487; Fat 28g; Sodium 669mg; Carbs 14g; Fibre 0g; Sugar 0g; Protein 54g

Caribbean-style Chicken Curry

Prep time: 15 minutes | Cook time: 6-8 hours | Serves: 6

1.3kg boneless, skin-on chicken thighs or other dark meat

1 onion, chopped

2 garlic cloves, minced

1 jalapeño pepper, chopped

120ml coconut milk

1 tablespoon curry powder

1 teaspoon allspice

½ teaspoon cloves

½ teaspoon nutmeg

1 teaspoon ground ginger

1. Add the chicken, onion, garlic, jalapeño, coconut milk, curry powder, allspice, cloves, nutmeg, and ginger to a slow cooker. Stir to mix well. 2. Cook on low temp setting for 6 to 8 hours.

Per Serving: Calories 360; Fat 26g; Sodium 663mg; Carbs 2g; Fibre 0g; Sugar 0g; Protein 27g

Prep time: 15 minutes | Cook time: 5-6 hours | Serves: 6

Nonstick cooking spray

900g boneless, skinless chicken breast, cut into 2.5cm pieces

1 (200g) can water chestnuts, drained

2 celery stalks, chopped

1 red pepper chopped

1 green pepper chopped

4 medium carrots, sliced

120ml plus 2 tablespoons water, divided

60ml low-sodium soy sauce

60ml balsamic vinegar

4 tablespoons sriracha sauce

4 garlic cloves, minced

2 tablespoons honey

1 tablespoon freshly grated ginger

1 tablespoon sesame oil

2 tablespoons cornflour

200g snow peas

1. Spray the slow cooker with the cooking spray. Add the chicken, water chestnuts, celery, peppers, and carrots. 2. In a bowl, whisk 120 ml water, the soy sauce, balsamic vinegar, sriracha, garlic, honey, ginger, and sesame oil. Pour this over the chicken and vegetables. Cover the slow cooker and cook on low temp setting for 5 to 6 hours. 3. About 20 minutes before serving, whisk the cornflour and remaining 2 tablespoons of water until the cornflour is dissolved. Stir this into the slow cooker along with the snow peas and continue cooking until sauce has thickened, 15 to 20 minutes. 4. Serve hot over rice or vegetables noodles garnished with chopped nuts and chopped spring onions, if desired.

Per Serving: Calories 887; Fat 71g; Sodium 874mg; Carbs 3g; Fibre 0g; Sugar 0g; Protein 59g

Prep time: 10 minutes | Cook time: 4-6 hours | Serves: 6

Cooking spray

900g boneless, skinless chicken breasts

200g uncured ham, sliced

200g Swiss cheese, sliced

420ml Cream of Mushroom Sauce

1 tablespoon unsalted butter, cut into small pieces

1. Coat a slow cooker with cooking spray. 2. Place the chicken in the bottom of the slow cooker. Place the ham slices over the chicken. Place the cheese on top. 3. Pour the mushroom sauce over the top and spread it evenly with a spoon. 4. Scatter the butter over the top. 5. Cook on low temp setting for 4 to 6 hours or on high for 2 to 3 hours.

Per Serving: Calories 293; Fat 11g; Sodium 856mg; Carbs 6g; Fibre 3g; Sugar 0g; Protein 41g

Chicken Provençal with White Beans & Olives

Prep time: 15 minutes | Cook time: 6-7 hours | Serves: 6

900g boneless, skinless chicken breasts

1 (200g) can no-salt-added diced tomatoes

480ml Chicken Stock

1 (375g) can cannellini beans, drained and rinsed

240ml white wine

2 onions, finely chopped

8 garlic cloves, minced

4 tablespoons tomato paste

2 tablespoons extra-virgin olive oil

2 teaspoons dried tarragon

2 teaspoons dried oregano

Freshly ground black pepper

Zest of 1 lemon

Juice of 1 lemon

90g Niçoise or Kalamata olives

15g fresh parsley, minced

1. Put the chicken, tomatoes, stock, beans, wine, onions, garlic, tomato paste, olive oil, tarragon, oregano, and black pepper in a slow cooker. Cover the slow cooker and cook on low temp setting for 6 to 7 hours, until chicken is cooked through. 2. Garnish the chicken and sauce with the lemon zest and juice, olives, and fresh parsley. Serve over rice, if desired.

Per Serving: Calories 355; Fat 25g; Sodium 647mg; Carbs 11g; Fibre 2g; Sugar 0.6g; Protein 22g

Coconut Lime Chicken with Sweet Potatoes

Prep time: 10 minutes | Cook time: 6-8 hours | Serves: 6

240ml water

4 garlic cloves, minced

1 tablespoon minced fresh ginger

Juice of 2 limes

1 teaspoon turmeric

1 teaspoon ground cumin

1 teaspoon curry powder

1 teaspoon ground coriander

Freshly ground black pepper

1.3kg boneless, skinless chicken breasts

530g sweet potato cubes

1 red pepper, chopped

30g chopped fresh coriander

1 (375g) can light coconut milk

1. Pour the water, garlic, ginger, and lime juice into the slow cooker and stir. 2. In a bowl, mix the turmeric, cumin, curry, coriander, and black pepper. Season the chicken with this spice mix, and add the chicken and spice mix to the slow cooker. 3. Top the chicken with the sweet potatoes, pepper, and coriander and stir to combine. 4. Cover the slow cooker and cook on low temp setting for 6 to 8 hours, until chicken is cooked through and the vegetables are tender. 5. Add the coconut milk to the slow cooker and stir to combine.3. Serve hot.

Per Serving: Calories 422; Fat 31g; Sodium 1101mg; Carbs 9g; Fibre 5g; Sugar 3g; Protein 28g

Sweet Chicken and Broccoli

Prep time: 10 minutes | Cook time: 5-6 hours | Serves: 6

Nonstick cooking spray

900g boneless, skinless chicken breasts, cut into 2.5cm pieces

310g frozen, shelled edamame

4 medium carrots, sliced

1 medium onion, chopped

120ml cold water

2 tablespoons cornflour

120ml Chicken Stock

1 tablespoon sesame oil or extra-virgin olive oil

4 garlic cloves, minced

60ml low-sodium soy sauce

70g honey

60g tomato paste

60ml rice wine vinegar

270g broccoli florets

4 tablespoons sesame seeds, for garnish

1. Spray a slow cooker with the cooking spray. Add the chicken, edamame, carrots, and onion. 2. In a bowl, whisk cold water and cornflour. Add the stock, sesame oil, garlic, soy sauce, honey, tomato paste, and vinegar and whisk to combine. Pour the sauce over chicken. 3. Cover the slow cooker and cook on low temp setting for 5 to 6 hours. In the last 30 minutes of cooking, stir in the broccoli and continue cooking until the vegetables are tender and the chicken is cooked through. 4. Serve hot, garnished with the sesame seeds. Serve over brown rice, if desired.

Per Serving: Calories 537; Fat 33g; Sodium 674mg; Carbs 9g; Fibre 4g; Sugar 1g; Protein 51g

One-Pot Whole Chicken with Thyme

Prep time: 15 minutes | Cook time: 7-8 hours | Serves: 8

60ml extra-virgin olive oil, divided

1 (1.3kg) whole chicken, washed and patted dry

Salt, for seasoning

Freshly ground black pepper, for Seasoning

1 lemon, litreered

6 thyme sprigs

4 garlic cloves, crushed

3 bay leaves

1 sweet onion, litreered

1. Lightly grease the slow cooker with 1 tablespoon of the olive oil. 2. Rub the remaining olive oil all over the chicken and spice with the salt and pepper. stuff the lemon litreers, thyme, garlic, and bay leaves into the cavity of the chicken. 3. Place the onion litreers on the bottom of the slow cooker and place the chicken on top so it does not touch the bottom of the. 4. Cover the slow cooker and cook on low temp setting for 7 to 8 hours. 5. Serve warm.

Per Serving: Calories 461; Fat 36g; Sodium 589mg; Carbs 18g; Fibre 7g; Sugar 2g; Protein 20g

Chocolaty Chicken Stew

Prep time: 15 minutes | Cook time: 7-8 hours | Serves: 6

3 tablespoons extra-virgin olive oil or ghee, divided

900g boneless chicken thighs and breasts

Salt, for seasoning

Freshly ground black pepper, for seasoning

1 sweet onion, chopped

1 tablespoon minced garlic

1 (200g) can diced tomatoes

4 dried chili peppers, soaked in water for 2 hours

and chopped

75g dark chocolate, chopped

25g natural peanut butter

1½ teaspoons ground cumin

¾ teaspoon ground cinnamon

½ teaspoon chili powder

120g coconut cream

2 tablespoons chopped coriander, for garnish

1. Lightly grease the slow cooker with 1 tablespoon of the olive oil. 2. In a frying pan over medium-high heat, heat the remaining 2 tablespoons of the olive oil. 3. Lightly spice the chicken with salt and pepper, add to the frying pan, and brown for about 5 minutes, turning once. 4. Add the onion and garlic and sauté for 3 minutes. 5. Transfer the chicken, onion, and garlic to the slow cooker, and stir in the tomatoes, chiles, chocolate, peanut butter, cumin, cinnamon, and chili powder. 6. Cover the slow cooker and cook on low temp setting for 7 to 8 hours. 7. Stir in the coconut cream, and serve hot, topped with the coriander.

Per Serving: Calories 456; Fat 31g; Sodium 775mg; Carbs 6g; Fibre 1g; Sugar 0.8g; Protein 37g

Coconut Chicken Stew

Prep time: 15 minutes | Cook time: 6-8 hours | Serves: 10

1 teaspoon rapeseed oil

2 medium onions, diced

4 cloves garlic, minced

3kg boneless, skinless chicken thighs, cubed

1 tablespoon minced fresh ginger

200g toasted unsweetened coconut

1 teaspoon ground cinnamon

¼ teaspoon ground nutmeg

½ teaspoon ground cloves

½ teaspoon salt

1 teaspoon cumin seeds

1 teaspoon black mustard seeds

2 tablespoons red pepper flakes

360ml water

1.In a frying pan, heat the oil. Add the onions and garlic and sauté them for 3 minutes. Place all ingredients in a slow cooker. Stir. Cover and cook for 6–8 hours on low temp setting. Stir before serving.

Per Serving: Calories 489; Fat 33g; Sodium 906mg; Carbs 2g; Fibre 0g; Sugar 0g; Protein 46g

Spiced Chicken

Prep time: 15 minutes | Cook time: 7-8 hours | Serves: 6

120ml extra-virgin olive oil, divided

900g boneless chicken (breast and thighs)

1 sweet onion, litreered

4 garlic cloves

2 spring onions, white and green parts, coarsely chopped

2 habanero chilies, stemmed and seeded

2 tablespoons granulated erythritol

1 tablespoon grated fresh ginger

2 teaspoons allspice

1 teaspoon dried thyme

½ teaspoon cardamom

½ teaspoon salt

2 tablespoons chopped coriander, for garnish

1. Lightly grease the slow cooker with 1 tablespoon of the olive oil. 2. arrange the chicken pieces in the bottom of the. 3. In a blender, pulse the remaining olive oil, onion, garlic, spring onion s, chiles, erythritol, ginger, allspice, thyme, cardamom, and salt until a thick, uniform sauce forms. 4. Pour the sauce over the chicken, turning the pieces to coat. 5. Cover the slow cooker and cook on low temp setting for 7 to 8 hours. 6. Serve topped with the coriander.

Per Serving: Calories 440; Fat 25g; Sodium 1020mg; Carbs 13g; Fibre 2g; Sugar 1g; Protein 40g

Delicious Chicken Thighs and Mushroom

Prep time: 15 minutes | Cook time: 8 hours | Serves: 6

3 tablespoons extra-virgin olive oil, divided

900g boneless chicken thighs

Salt, for seasoning

Freshly ground black pepper, for Seasoning

1 (350g) can stewed tomatoes

480ml chicken stock

100g litreered button mushrooms

½ sweet onion, chopped

1 tablespoon minced garlic

1 tablespoon dried oregano

1 teaspoon dried basil

Pinch red pepper flakes

1. Lightly grease the slow cooker with 1 tablespoon of the olive oil. 2. Lightly spice the chicken thighs with salt and pepper. 3. In a frying pan over medium-high heat, heat the remaining 2 tablespoons of the olive oil. Add the chicken thighs and brown for about 8 minutes, turning once. 4. Transfer the chicken to the slow cooker and add the tomatoes, stock, mushrooms, onion, garlic, oregano, basil, and red pepper flakes. 5. Cover the slow cooker and cook on low temp setting for 8 hours. 6. Serve warm.

Per Serving: Calories 452; Fat 32g; Sodium 932mg; Carbs 1g; Fibre 0g; Sugar 0g; Protein 40g

Cream Chicken Lettuce Tacos

Prep time: 10 minutes | Cook time: 6 hours | Serves: 6

55g unsalted butter, melted

150g diced tomatoes

190g halved green olives

½ onion, diced

2 garlic cloves, minced

1 or 2 jalapeño peppers, seeded and minced

1½ tablespoons chili powder

1½ teaspoons ground cumin

1 teaspoon dried oregano

1 teaspoon paprika

½ teaspoon salt

¼ teaspoon freshly ground black pepper

675g boneless, skinless chicken thighs

240g sour cream

12 lettuce leaves

200g grated Cheddar cheese

2 avocados, peeled, pitted, and sliced

1. In the slow cooker, stir the butter, tomatoes, olives, onion, garlic, jalapeños, chili powder, cumin, oregano, paprika, salt, and pepper. 2. Place the chicken pieces in the cooker and stir to coat them in the sauce. Cover and cook for 6 hours on low temp setting. 3. Transfer the chicken pieces to a bowl or work surface. Using two forks, shred the chicken and then return the grated meat to the slow cooker. 4. Stir in the sour cream. 5. To serve, spoon the chicken mixture into the lettuce leaves and garnish with Cheddar cheese and avocado slices.

Per Serving: Calories 490; Fat 34g; Sodium 951mg; Carbs 12g; Fibre 3g; Sugar 1g; Protein 35g

Tangy Orange Chicken

Prep time: 10 minutes | Cook time: 3 hours | Serves: 4

2 tablespoons soy sauce

2 tablespoons spiced ginger preserves or orange marmalade

1 teaspoon ground ginger (if orange marmalade is

used)

120ml freshly squeezed orange juice

1 orange, cut into ½ cm thick slices

3 boneless, skinless chicken breasts (about 455g)

1. In a bowl, whisk the soy sauce, preserves, ginger, and orange juice. 2. Arrange the orange slices along the bottom of a slow cooker. Top with the chicken breasts. Pour the sauce over the chicken. 3. Cook for 3 hours on low temp setting until the chicken is thoroughly cooked.

Per Serving: Calories 527; Fat 44g; Sodium 766mg; Carbs 2g; Fibre 0g; Sugar 0g; Protein 29g

Asian-Style Orange Chicken

Prep time: 10 minutes | Cook time: 6 hours | Serves: 6

675g bone-in, skin-on chicken thighs

1 tablespoon Chinese five-spice powder

½ teaspoon salt

6 bacon slices, diced

1 orange, sliced

1 small red chili pepper, very thinly sliced, or ½ teaspoon red pepper flakes

1 garlic clove, minced

1 tablespoon minced fresh ginger

60g Asian sesame paste

2 tablespoons soy sauce or tamari

1 tablespoon freshly squeezed lime juice

1 tablespoon toasted sesame oil

1 tablespoon erythritol

55g unsalted butter, cubed

60g chopped macadamia nuts

1. Season the chicken thighs all over with the five-spice powder and salt. Set aside. 2. In a frying pan, cook the bacon over medium-high heat until crisp and browned, about 5 minutes. Transfer the bacon to the slow cooker. 3. Add the orange slices, red chili pepper, garlic, ginger, sesame paste, soy sauce, lime juice, sesame oil, and erythritol. Stir to mix. 4. Return to the frying pan at medium-high heat and add the spiced chicken, skin-side down. Cook until browned, about 3 minutes per side. Arrange the browned chicken in the slow cooker, skin-side up. Top with the butter pieces. Cover and cook for 6 hours on low temp setting. Serve hot, garnished with the macadamia nuts.

Per Serving: Calories 389; Fat 24g; Sodium 855mg; Carbs 6g; Fibre 1g; Sugar 0g; Protein 30g

Gingered Chicken Thighs

Prep time: 10 minutes | Cook time: 2½ hours | Serves: 4

4 boneless, skinless chicken thighs

3 tablespoons soy sauce

3 tablespoons chicken or vegetable stock

3 tablespoons lime juice

1 knob ginger, minced (or 1 teaspoon ground ginger)

1 shallot, thinly sliced

2 cloves garlic, thinly sliced

¼ teaspoon white pepper

1. Place all ingredients into a slow cooker. Cook on high temp setting for 2½ hours. Discard the cooking liquid before serving.

Per Serving: Calories 451; Fat 27g; Sodium 852mg; Carbs 10g; Fibre 3g; Sugar 0g; Protein 42g

Chicken Meatballs with Tropical Sauce

Prep time: 15 minutes | Cook time: 4-6 hours | Serves: 15

Sauce

Nonstick cooking spray

1 tablespoon vegetable oil

1 onion, minced

1 tablespoon minced jalapeño pepper

1 tablespoon grated fresh ginger

240ml pineapple juice

70g packed dark brown sugar

60g teriyaki sauce

60ml ponzu sauce

3 tablespoons lime juice

1 tablespoon cornflour

980g frozen pineapple chunks

Meatballs

900g chicken mince breast

1 teaspoon ground ginger

50g bread crumbs

1 egg

30g minced onion

2 cloves garlic, minced

1. Spray the inside of slow cooker with cooking spray. Heat the vegetable oil over medium-high heat in a 3- or 4-litre saucepan. When hot, add the onion, jalapeño, and ginger. Cook, stirring frequently, until the onion becomes translucent, about 5 minutes. 2. Add the pineapple juice, brown sugar, teriyaki sauce, and ponzu sauce. 3. Mix the lime juice with the cornflour and whisk into the sauce. Stir in the pineapple chunks and bring the sauce to a boil. 4. While sauce is heating, mix the chicken, ground ginger, bread crumbs, egg, minced onion, and garlic in a bowl. Form the mixture into 1" balls and place in prepared cooker. 5. Pour sauce over meatballs. Cover the slow cooker and cook on low temp setting for 4–6 hours or until meatballs are no longer pink in the centre.

Per Serving: Calories 463; Fat 30g; Sodium 995mg; Carbs 8g; Fibre 1g; Sugar 0.8g; Protein 39g

Spicy Teriyaki Chicken

Prep time: 10 minutes | Cook time: 1 hour | Serves: 6

455g frozen chicken nuggets, defrosted

125 – 150g teriyaki sauce

1 teaspoon hot sauce

In a slow cooker, combine all ingredients and cook over low temp setting for 1 hour. Serve hot.

Per Serving: Calories 242; Fat 15.16g; Sodium 818mg; Carbs 14.03g; Fiber 0.9g; Sugar 3.37g; Protein 12.25g

Indian Chicken and Chickpea Curry

Prep time: 10 minutes | Cook time: 4-6 hours | Serves: 4

Nonstick spray

1 tablespoon olive oil

2 medium onions, finely chopped

3 garlic cloves, minced

1 teaspoon ground ginger

½ teaspoon turmeric

2 teaspoons sweet paprika

2 teaspoons curry powder

1 (300g) can chicken stock, low-sodium preferred

1 (360g) can chickpeas, drained and rinsed

10g packed fresh coriander leaves, coarsely chopped

4 boneless, skinless chicken breasts

Hot cooked rice

1. Spray the slow cooker with spray. Heat the oil over medium-high heat in a frying pan. When hot, add the onions and cook, for about 5 minutes or until they begin to brown. 2. Add the garlic, ginger, turmeric, paprika, and curry powder; stir continuously for 1 minute or until fragrant. 3. Add the chicken stock, and chickpeas; bring the mixture to a boil. Once the sauce has reached a boil, mash some of the chickpeas with the back of a wooden spoon or potato masher to help thicken sauce. 4. Add the coriander and remove from the heat. Place the chicken in the prepared cooker. 5. Pour the chickpea mixture over the chicken. Cover and cook on high temp setting for 2–3 hours or low for 4–6 hours. 6. If sauce is too thin, uncover and continue to cook on high temp setting for another 30 minutes. Serve over hot cooked rice.

Per Serving: Calories 275; Fat 17g; Sodium 974mg; Carbs 3g; Fibre 1g; Sugar 1g; Protein 28g

Creamy Cheese Chicken & Bacon Casserole

Prep time: 10 minutes | Cook time: 4-6 hours | Serves: 6

1.3kg boneless, skinless chicken thighs

100g bacon, cooked and crumbled

200g low-fat cream cheese

200g low-fat sour cream

200g Cheddar cheese, grated

30g diced onion

1 teaspoon garlic powder

1 teaspoon parsley

½ teaspoon salt

¼ teaspoon freshly ground black pepper

1. Add the chicken, bacon, cream cheese, sour cream, Cheddar, onion, garlic powder, parsley, salt, and pepper to a slow cooker. Stir to mix well. 2. Cook on low temp setting for 4 for 6 hours or on high for 2 to 3 hours.

Per Serving: Calories 677; Fat 61g; Sodium 822mg; Carbs 8g; Fibre 0g; Sugar 0g; Protein 26g

Creamy Chicken and Mushroom

Prep time: 10 minutes | Cook time: 8 hours | Serves: 6

½ onion, thinly sliced

675g boneless, skinless chicken thighs

1 teaspoon salt

½ teaspoon freshly ground black pepper

3 tablespoons sweet Hungarian paprika

200g cremini or button mushrooms, sliced

55g unsalted butter, melted

120ml chicken stock or water

2 tablespoons tomato paste

1 garlic clove, minced

⅓ teaspoon cayenne pepper

480g sour cream

1. Cover the bottom of the slow cooker with the onion slices. 2. Season the chicken pieces all over with the salt, pepper, and paprika. Arrange the chicken on top of the onions. 3. Scatter the mushrooms over the chicken and drizzle the melted butter over the top. 4. In a bowl, whisk the chicken stock, tomato paste, garlic, and cayenne. Pour this sauce over the chicken. Cover and cook for 8 hours on low temp setting. 5. Transfer the chicken pieces to a bowl and shred the meat using two forks. 6. Stir the sour cream into the sauce in the slow cooker until well incorporated. Return the chicken meat to the slow cooker and stir to mix. Serve hot.

Per Serving: Calories 459; Fat 35g; Sodium 687mg; Carbs 7g; Fibre 2g; Sugar 0g; Protein 29g

Cheesy Ranch Chicken with Bacon

Prep time: 10 minutes | Cook time: 4-6 hours | Serves: 8

900g boneless, skinless chicken breasts

120ml water

200g low-fat cream cheese

2 tablespoons Homemade Ranch Seasoning

6 slices bacon, cooked and chopped

100g grated low-fat Cheddar cheese

1. Add the chicken, water, and cream cheese to a slow cooker. Sprinkle the ranch Seasoning on top. Stir to mix well. 2. Cook on low temp setting for 4 to 6 hours or on high for 2 to 3 hours. 3. Remove the chicken and shred it using two forks. 4. Add the chicken back into the slow cooker along with the bacon. Stir to mix well. Top with the Cheddar cheese and serve.

Per Serving: Calories 407; Fat 31g; Sodium 770mg; Carbs 3g; Fibre 0g; Sugar 0g; Protein 27g

Prep time: 15 minutes | Cook time: 3-4 hours | Serves: 8

1 tablespoon vegetable oil

1 medium yellow onion, peeled and diced

1 small green pepper, finely chopped

1 small red pepper, finely chopped

2 garlic cloves, minced

1 (300g) package sweet Italian sausages, cut on the diagonal into ¼" slices

3 skinless, boneless chicken breasts (approximately 675g), cut into 1 cm wide strips

1 teaspoon salt

¼ teaspoon cayenne pepper

¼ teaspoon black pepper

1 bay leaf

1 (375g) can diced tomatoes, drained

480ml chicken stock

800g cooked rice

10g loosely packed parsley leaves

1. Heat oil in a frying pan over medium-high heat. Add onion and peppers and sauté, for 5 minutes or until onion begins to brown. Add garlic and stir for another 30 seconds. 2. Transfer vegetables to the slow cooker. Add sausage slices to the frying pan. Let brown without stirring for 2 minutes each side. 3. Transfer sausage slices to the slow cooker. Top with chicken, then add remaining ingredients except rice and parsley. 4. Cover the slow cooker and cook on low temp setting for 6–8 hours or on high for 3–4 hours. Discard bay leaf. 5. Serve over rice, garnished with parsley leaves.

Per Serving: Calories 607; Fat 52g; Sodium 741mg; Carbs 13g; Fibre 5g; Sugar 2g; Protein 25g

Chapter 5 Beef, Pork and Lamb

Spicy Beef Short Ribs

Prep time: 10 minutes | Cook time: 7-8 hours | Serves: 8

1 tablespoon extra-virgin olive oil

900g beef short ribs

1 sweet onion, sliced

480ml beef stock

2 tablespoons granulated erythritol

2 tablespoons balsamic vinegar

2 teaspoons dried thyme

1 teaspoon hot sauce

1. Lightly grease the slow cooker with the olive oil. 2. Place the ribs, onion, stock, erythritol, balsamic vinegar, thyme, and hot sauce in the slow cooker. 3. Cover the slow cooker and cook on low temp setting for 7 to 8 hours. 4. Serve warm.

Per Serving: Calories 675; Fat 51g; Sodium 763mg; Carbs 5g; Fibre 1g; Sugar 1g; Protein 49g

Creamy Swiss Steak

Prep time: 10 minutes | Cook time: 9 hours | Serves: 6

120ml chicken stock

2 medium yellow onions, halved and thinly sliced

1 (360g) can petite diced tomatoes

675g white mushrooms, sliced

1 teaspoon dried thyme

6 (200g) beef blade steaks

½ teaspoon salt, plus more for seasoning

¼ teaspoon freshly ground black pepper, plus more for seasoning

80g double cream

2 tablespoons minced fresh parsley

1. Combine the stock, onions, tomatoes with their juice, mushrooms, and thyme in the slow cooker. Place the beef on top of the vegetables. Sprinkle with the salt and pepper. 2. Cover the slow cooker and cook on low temp setting for 9 hours until the beef is tender. 3. Transfer the steaks to a platter and tent them loosely with aluminum foil. Let the liquid in the slow cooker settle for 5 minutes, then skim off and discard the extra fat from the surface using a spoon. Stir in the cream and parsley, and Spice with salt and pepper, if desired. 4. Serve the steaks with the sauce.

Per Serving: Calories 243; Fat 15g; Sodium 632mg; Carbs 2g; Fibre 0.5g; Sugar 0.1g; Protein 25g

Cheese Beef Sandwiches

Prep time: 10 minutes | Cook time: 8 hours | Serves: 6

1 (900g) beef chuck roast, trimmed of excess fat

½ teaspoon salt, plus more for seasoning

¼ teaspoon freshly ground black pepper, plus more for seasoning

720ml beef stock

60ml Worcestershire sauce

2 yellow onions, very thinly sliced

2 teaspoons garlic powder

1 bay leaf

6 crusty French rolls, toasted if desired

8 slices provolone cheese

1. Put the beef in the slow cooker. Sprinkle with the salt and pepper. Add the stock, Worcestershire sauce, onions, garlic powder, and bay leaf. 2. Cover the slow cooker and cook on low temp setting for 8 hours until the beef is very tender. 3. Transfer the beef to a cutting board. Slice or shred the meat. Season with salt and pepper, if needed. 4. Place a fine-mesh strainer over a bowl and pour the juices from the slow cooker through the strainer and into the bowl. This juice will be the "au jus," or dipping sauce. 5. Pile the meat on the bottoms of the rolls and add some onions on top of the meat. Place a slice of cheese on top of the onions, if desired. 6. Serve the sandwiches with a bowl of the reserved dipping sauce.

Per Serving: Calories 307; Fat 25g; Sodium 633mg; Carbs 7.5g; Fibre 2.5g; Sugar 1g; Protein 13g

Flank Steak Tacos

Prep time: 10 minutes | Cook time: 8-10 hours | Serves: 8

1 red onion, sliced thin

1.3kg flank steak, trimmed of fat

105g honey

60ml rice wine vinegar

4 garlic cloves, minced

1 jalapeño pepper, seeded and finely diced

3 tablespoons low-sodium soy sauce or tamari

2 tablespoons minced fresh ginger

1 tablespoon sesame oil

16 (15cm) corn tortillas

180g finely grated cabbage, for garnish

30g chopped fresh coriander, for garnish

Sriracha sauce, for garnish

1. Place the onion on the bottom of a slow cooker. Add the steak, honey, vinegar, garlic, jalapeño, soy sauce, ginger, and sesame oil. Cover the slow cooker and cook on low temp setting for 8 to 10 hours. 2. Shred the beef with a pair of forks and stir it into the liquid in the slow cooker. 3. Serve the beef in the corn tortillas. If desired, garnish with grated cabbage, coriander, and sriracha sauce.

Per Serving: Calories 385; Fat 29g; Sodium 781mg; Carbs 3g; Fibre 1g; Sugar 1g; Protein 28g

Beef, Cabbage and Rice Casserole

Prep time: 10 minutes | Cook time: 7-8 hours | Serves: 8

1 tablespoon extra-virgin olive oil

675g 93% lean beef mince

1 onion, chopped

4 garlic cloves, minced

Nonstick cooking spray

300g brown rice

1 medium head green cabbage, cored and chopped

480g Rustic Marinara Sauce

1 (360g) can no-salt-added diced tomatoes

280g Spicy Salsa

240ml Beef Stock

1 pepper (any colour), chopped

1 teaspoon smoked paprika

1 teaspoon dried thyme

1. Spray the slow cooker with the cooking spray. Place the rice in the bottom of the slow cooker followed by half of the cabbage. 2. Add the beef and vegetables over the cabbage layer. 3. Add the remaining cabbage along with the marinara, tomatoes, salsa, stock, pepper, paprika, and thyme. Cover the slow cooker and cook on low temp setting for 7 to 8 hours, until the rice is cooked and the vegetables are tender. 4. Serve hot.

Per Serving: Calories 460; Fat 36g; Sodium 661mg; Carbs 11g; Fibre 5g; Sugar 2g; Protein 23g

Delicious Beef and Spring Vegetables Stew

Prep time: 15 minutes | Cook time: 7-8 hours | Serves: 8

675g lean beef roast, cut into bite-size cubes

2 tablespoons plain flour

2 tablespoons extra-virgin olive oil, divided

4 garlic cloves, minced

200g halved button mushrooms

2 leeks, white and light green parts, sliced thinly

2 carrots, sliced thinly

360ml dry red wine

360ml Beef Stock

455g small red potatoes

2 teaspoons dried thyme

1 teaspoon dried rosemary

180g chopped asparagus

1. Toss the beef cubes with the flour and 1 tablespoon olive oil. 2. Transfer the beef to the slow cooker. Return the frying pan to the heat, add the remaining 1 tablespoon of oil. Add the garlic, mushrooms, leeks, and carrots and cook until the vegetables begin to soften, 3 to 5 minutes. Transfer the vegetables to the slow cooker. If not browning these ingredients, just put them all directly into the slow cooker. 3. Add the wine, stock (or stock), potatoes, thyme, and rosemary to the slow cooker. Cover the slow cooker and cook on low temp setting for 7 to 8 hours. In the last 30 minutes, add the asparagus and continue cooking until crisp tender. 4. Serve hot.

Per Serving: Calories 379; Fat 29g; Sodium 722mg; Carbs 2.5g; Fibre 0g; Sugar 0g; Protein 27g

Creamy Lime Beef

Prep time: 15 minutes | Cook time: 9-10 hours | Serves: 8

120ml extra-virgin olive oil, divided

60ml lime juice

2 tablespoons apple cider vinegar

2 teaspoons minced garlic

1½ teaspoons paprika

1 teaspoon ground cumin

1 teaspoon chili powder

¼ teaspoon cayenne pepper

1 sweet onion cut into eighths

900g beef rump roast

240g sour cream, for garnish

1. Lightly grease the slow cooker with 1 tablespoon of the olive oil. 2. In a bowl, whisk the remaining olive oil, lime juice, apple cider vinegar, garlic, paprika, cumin, chili powder, and cayenne until well blended. 3. Place the onion in the bottom of the pot and the beef on top of the vegetable. Pour the sauce over the beef. 4. Cover the slow cooker and cook on low temp setting for 9 to 10 hours. 5. Shred the beef with a fork. 6. Serve topped with the sour cream.

Per Serving: Calories 339; Fat 19g; Sodium 489mg; Carbs 6g; Fibre 0.5g; Sugar 0g; Protein 36g

Delicious Cheese Stuffed Meatballs

Prep time: 30 minutes | Cook time: 5-6 hours | Serves: 6

3 tablespoons extra-virgin olive oil, divided

675g beef mince

1 egg

25g grated Parmesan cheese

2 teaspoons minced garlic

2 teaspoons dried basil

½ teaspoon salt

¼ teaspoon freshly ground black pepper

150g mozzarella, cut into 16 small cubes

960g simple marinara sauce

1. Lightly grease the slow cooker with the olive oil. 2. In bowl, combine the beef, egg, parmesan, garlic, basil, salt, and pepper until well mixed. Shape the mixture into 16 meatballs and press a mozzarella piece into the centre of each, making sure to completely enclose the cheese. 3. In a frying pan over medium-high heat, heat the remaining 2 tablespoons of the olive oil. add the meatballs and brown all over, about 10 minutes. 4. Transfer the meatballs to the cooker and add the marinara sauce. 5. Cover the slow cooker and cook on low temp setting for 5 to 6 hours. 6. Serve warm.

Per Serving: Calories 256; Fat 20g; Sodium 777mg; Carbs 1g; Fibre 0g; Sugar 0g; Protein 18g

Spicy Beef Goulash

Prep time: 15 minutes | Cook time: 9-10 hours | Serves: 6

1 tablespoon extra-virgin olive oil

675g beef, cut into 2.5 cm pieces

½ sweet onion, chopped

1 carrot, cut into 1 cm-thick slices

1 red pepper, diced

2 teaspoons minced garlic

240ml beef stock

60g tomato paste

1 tablespoon Hungarian paprika

1 bay leaf

240g sour cream

2 tablespoons chopped fresh parsley, for garnish

1. Lightly grease the slow cooker with the olive oil. 2. Add the beef, onion, carrot, red pepper, garlic, stock, tomato paste, paprika, and bay leaf to the. 3. Cover the slow cooker and cook on low temp setting for 9 to 10 hours. 4. Remove the bay leaf and stir in the sour cream. 5. Serve topped with the parsley.

Per Serving: Calories 435; Fat 23g; Sodium 880mg; Carbs 0g; Fibre 0g; Sugar 0g; Protein 57g

Tangy Balsamic Roast Beef

Prep time: 15 minutes | Cook time: 7-8 hours | Serves: 8

3 tablespoons of extra-virgin olive oil, divided

900g boneless beef chuck roast

240ml beef stock

120ml balsamic vinegar

1 tablespoon minced garlic

1 tablespoon granulated erythritol

½ teaspoon red pepper flakes

1 tablespoon chopped fresh thyme

1. Lightly grease the slow cooker with 1 tablespoon of the olive oil. 2. In a frying pan over medium-high heat, heat the remaining 2 tablespoons of the olive oil. add the beef and brown on all sides, about 7 minutes total. transfer to the slow cooker. 3. In a bowl, whisk the stock, balsamic vinegar, garlic, erythritol, red pepper flakes, and thyme until blended. 4. Pour the sauce over the beef. 5. Cover the slow cooker and cook on low temp setting for 7 to 8 hours. 6. Serve warm.

Per Serving: Calories 480; Fat 32g; Sodium 789mg; Carbs 12g; Fibre 3g; Sugar 1g; Protein 36g

Coconut Curry Beef with Bok Choy

Prep time: 10 minutes | Cook time: 7-8 hours | Serves: 6

1 tablespoon extra-virgin olive oil

455g beef chuck roast, cut into 5cm pieces

1 sweet onion, chopped

1 red pepper, diced

480ml coconut milk

2 tablespoons hot curry powder

1 tablespoon coconut aminos

2 teaspoons grated fresh ginger

2 teaspoons minced garlic

90g grated baby bok choy

1. Lightly grease the slow cooker with the olive oil. 2. Add the beef, onion, and pepper. 3. In a bowl, whisk the coconut milk, curry, coconut aminos, ginger, and garlic. Pour the sauce into the and stir to combine. 4. Cover the slow cooker and cook on low temp setting for 7 to 8 hours. 5. Stir in the bok choy and let stand 15 minutes. 6. Serve warm.

Per Serving: Calories 354; Fat 24g; Sodium 894mg; Carbs 1g; Fibre 0g; Sugar 0g; Protein 31g

Beef & Cabbage in Cheese Marinara Sauce

Prep time: 15 minutes | Cook time: 7-8 hours | Serves: 4

3 tablespoons extra-virgin olive oil, divided

455g beef mince

1 sweet onion, chopped

180g finely chopped cauliflower

2 teaspoons minced garlic

1 teaspoon dried thyme

¼ teaspoon salt

¼ teaspoon freshly ground black pepper

360g grated cabbage

480g simple marinara sauce

120g cream cheese

1. Lightly grease the slow cooker with 1 tablespoon of the olive oil. 2. Press the beef mince along bottom of the slow cooker. 3. In a medium frying pan over medium-high heat, heat the remaining 2 tablespoons of the olive oil. Add the onion, cauliflower, garlic, thyme, salt, and pepper, and sauté until the onion is softened, about 3 minutes. 4. Add the cabbage and sauté for an 5 minutes. 5. Transfer the cabbage mixture to the slow cooker, pour the marinara sauce over the cabbage, and top with the cream cheese. 6. Cover the slow cooker and cook on low temp setting for 7 to 8 hours. 7. Stir before serving.

Per Serving: Calories 739; Fat 63g; Sodium 652mg; Carbs 7g; Fibre 2g; Sugar 1g; Protein 35g

Tropical Lemongrass Pork

Prep time: 10 minutes | Cook time: 8 hours | Serves: 6

60ml coconut oil, melted

1 tablespoon apple cider vinegar

3 tablespoons minced lemongrass (white part only)

3 garlic cloves, minced

2 teaspoons salt

1 teaspoon freshly ground black pepper

900g boneless pork shoulder or butt roast, top fatty layer scored in a crisscross pattern

1 onion, sliced

1 (5cm) piece fresh ginger, peeled and cut into thin slices

1 (350g) can coconut milk

1. In a bowl, stir the coconut oil, cider vinegar, lemongrass, garlic, salt, and pepper. 2. Place the pork in a baking dish and rub the Seasoning mixture all over it. Cover and refrigerate overnight. 3. Cover the bottom of the slow cooker with the onion and ginger slices in an even layer. 4. Top with the marinated pork, along with any accumulated juices in the dish. 5. Pour the coconut milk over the top. Cover and cook for 8 hours on low temp setting. 6. Shred the meat using two forks. Serve immediately.

Per Serving: Calories 352; Fat 29g; Sodium 458mg; Carbs 5g; Fibre 2g; Sugar 1g; Protein 17g

Spiced Pork Belly with Brussels Sprouts & Turnips

Prep time: 10 minutes | Cook time: 8 hours | Serves: 6-8

2 tablespoons paprika

2 tablespoons onion powder

2 tablespoons garlic powder

1 tablespoon salt

1 tablespoon freshly ground black pepper

900g pork belly, thickly sliced

455g Brussels sprouts, halved

1 medium turnip, peeled and diced

4 bay leaves

1. In a bowl, stir the paprika, onion powder, garlic powder, salt, and pepper. Rub the mixture all over the pork belly slices. 2. In the bottom of the slow cooker, arrange the Brussels sprouts, turnip, and bay leaves in an even layer. 3. Lay the pork over the vegetables. Cover and cook for 8 hours on low temp setting. 4. Discard the bay leaves and serve hot.

Per Serving: Calories 568; Fat 47g; Sodium 999mg; Carbs 11g; Fibre 3g; Sugar 2g; Protein 26g

Creamy Pork & Sausage Meatballs

Prep time: 20 minutes | Cook time: 8 hours | Serves: 4

For the Meatballs

675g sweet Italian sausage, casings removed

200g pork mince

100g almond meal

60g pine nuts

200g finely grated Parmesan cheese, divided

For the Sauce

55g unsalted butter, melted

1 (360g) can diced tomatoes, with juice

60g tomato paste

15g dried porcini mushrooms, crumbled

1 teaspoon dried oregano

1 egg, beaten

1 teaspoon rubbed sage

1 teaspoon dried oregano

½ teaspoon salt

¼ teaspoon freshly grated nutmeg

1 teaspoon dried thyme

½ teaspoon fennel seeds

½ teaspoon salt

¼ teaspoon red pepper flakes

240g double cream

1. In a bowl, thoroughly mix the sausage, pork mince, almond meal, and pine nuts. 2. Add 100g of Parmesan cheese, egg, sage, oregano, salt, and nutmeg. Mix well. Form the mixture into 12 meatballs. 3. In the slow cooker, stir the butter, tomatoes and their juice, tomato paste, mushrooms, oregano, thyme, fennel seeds, salt, and red pepper flakes. Nestle the meatballs in the sauce. Cover and cook for 8 hours on low temp setting. 4. Just before serving, stir in the double cream. Serve hot, garnished with the remaining Parmesan cheese.

Per Serving: Calories 600; Fat 52g; Sodium 741mg; Carbs 12g; Fibre 4g; Sugar 2g; Protein 22g

Tender Steak Stew

Prep time: 5 minutes | Cook time: 4-6 hours | Serves: 6

900g beef stew meat

120ml Bone Stock

15g steak Seasoning

2 tablespoons unsalted butter

1 tablespoon dried chopped onion

1 garlic clove, minced

¼ teaspoon salt (optional, if steak Seasoning doesn't include it)

1.Add the beef, stock, steak Seasoning, butter, dried onion, garlic, and salt to a slow cooker. Stir to mix well. 2. Cook on low temp setting for 4 to 6 hours or on high for 2 to 3 hours.

Per Serving: Calories 460; Fat 36g; Sodium 661mg; Carbs 11g; Fibre 5g; Sugar 2g; Protein 23g

Tangy Mustard-Herb Pork Chops

Prep time: 5 minutes | Cook time: 8 hours | Serves: 4

180ml chicken or beef stock

2 tablespoons coconut oil, melted

1 tablespoon Dijon mustard

2 garlic cloves, minced

1 tablespoon paprika

1 tablespoon onion powder

1 teaspoon dried oregano

1 teaspoon dried basil

1 teaspoon dried parsley

1 onion, thinly sliced

4 thick-cut boneless pork chops

240g double cream

1. In the slow cooker, stir the stock, coconut oil, mustard, garlic, paprika, onion powder, oregano, basil, and parsley.
2. Add the onion and pork chops and toss to coat. Cover and cook for 8 hours on low temp. 3. Transfer the chops to a serving platter. Transfer the remaining juices and onion in the slow cooker to a blender, add the double cream, and process until smooth. Pour the sauce over the pork chops and serve hot.

Per Serving: Calories 390; Fat 34g; Sodium 712mg; Carbs 2g; Fibre 1g; Sugar 1g; Protein 19g

Pork Loin with Creamy Gravy

Prep time: 10 minutes | Cook time: 8 hours | Serves: 6

1 tablespoon salt

2 teaspoons freshly ground black pepper

4 garlic cloves, minced

1 (1.3kg) bone-in pork loin roast

2 onions, sliced

60ml water

2 tablespoons soy sauce or tamari

240g double cream

1. In a bowl, stir the salt, pepper, and garlic to form a paste. Rub the Seasoning mixture all over the pork roast. 2. Arrange the onions in the bottom of the slow cooker. Pour in the water and soy sauce. Place the roast on top of the onions. Cover and cook for 8 hours on low temp setting. 3. Remove the roast from the slow cooker and let it rest for 10 minutes. 4. While the roast is resting, transfer the remaining liquid and onions from the slow cooker to a blender. Add the double cream and process into a smooth sauce. 5. Slice the pork and serve it with the gravy spooned over the top.

Per Serving: Calories 489; Fat 40g; Sodium 861mg; Carbs 9g; Fibre 1g; Sugar 2g; Protein 23g

Corned Beef & Cabbage with Horseradish Cream

Prep time: 10 minutes | Cook time: 8 hours | Serves: 8-10

For the Horseradish Cream

360g sour cream

225g prepared horseradish

2 tablespoons Dijon mustard

1½ teaspoons white wine vinegar

1 teaspoon salt

½ teaspoon freshly ground black pepper

For the Beef

1 head cabbage, cut into wedges

1 onion, chopped

110g unsalted butter or Ghee (here), melted

360ml water

½ teaspoon ground coriander

½ teaspoon ground mustard

½ teaspoon ground allspice

½ teaspoon ground marjoram

½ teaspoon ground thyme

½ teaspoon salt

½ teaspoon freshly ground black pepper

1 (1.3kg) corned beef brisket

1. In the slow cooker, toss the cabbage wedges, onion, and butter, and then spread them out in an even layer. Add the water. 2. In a bowl, stir the coriander, mustard, allspice, marjoram, thyme, salt, and pepper. Rub the spice mixture all over the corned beef. Place the beef on top of the vegetables in the slow cooker. Cover and cook for 8 hours on low temp setting. 3. Let the meat rest for 5 to 10 minutes before slicing. Serve with the vegetables and horseradish cream.

Per Serving: Calories 500; Fat 42g; Sodium 1032mg; Carbs 9g; Fibre 2g; Sugar 2g; Protein 23g

Tangy Beef and Olive

Prep time: 5 minutes | Cook time: 6-8 hours | Serves: 4

455g 93% lean beef mince

75g low-sodium or no-salt-added diced tomatoes

90g pimento-stuffed green olives

½ tablespoon capers

½ small onion, diced

1 tablespoon tomato paste

½ teaspoon ground cumin

¼ teaspoon salt

⅛ teaspoon freshly ground black pepper

1. Add the beef mince, tomatoes, olives, capers, onion, tomato paste, cumin, salt, and pepper to a slow cooker. Stir to mix well. 2. Cook on low temp setting for 6 to 8 hours or on high for 3 to 4 hours.

Per Serving: Calories 385; Fat 29g; Sodium 781mg; Carbs 3g; Fibre 1g; Sugar 1g; Protein 28g

Pork Loin with Gingery Cream Sauce

Prep time: 15 minutes | Cook time: 8 hours | Serves: 2

For the Pork

1 tablespoon erythritol

2 teaspoons salt

1 teaspoon garlic powder

1 teaspoon ground ginger

½ teaspoon ground cinnamon

½ teaspoon ground cloves

½ teaspoon red pepper flakes

¼ teaspoon freshly ground black pepper

1 (900g) pork shoulder roast

120ml water

For the Sauce

2 tablespoons unsalted butter

3 tablespoons minced fresh ginger

2 shallots, minced

1 tablespoon minced garlic

160ml dry white wine

240g double cream

1. In a bowl, stir the erythritol, salt, garlic powder, ginger, cinnamon, cloves, red pepper flakes, and black pepper. Rub the seasoning mixture all over the pork and place it in the slow cooker. 2. Pour the water into the cooker around the pork. Cover and cook for 8 hours on low temp setting. 3. Remove the pork from the slow cooker and let it rest for about 5 minutes. 4. While the pork rests, melt the butter in a small saucepan over medium heat. 5. Stir in the ginger, shallots, and garlic. 6. Add the white wine and bring to a boil. Cook, stirring, until the liquid is reduced to about 60ml about 5 minutes. 7. Whisk in the double cream and continue to boil, stirring, until the sauce thickens, 3 to 5 minutes more. 8. Slice the pork and serve it with the sauce spooned over the top.

Per Serving: Calories 530; Fat 48g; Sodium 661mg; Carbs 7g; Fibre 5g; Sugar 1g; Protein 20g

Cheesy Beef Enchilada Casserole

Prep time: 10 minutes | Cook time: 4-6 hours | Serves: 6

455g 93% lean beef mince

250g riced cauliflower

480g enchilada sauce

1 teaspoon chili powder

1 teaspoon paprika

½ teaspoon garlic powder

⅛ teaspoon freshly ground black pepper

100g diced green chiles

100g low-fat cream cheese

200g grated Cheddar cheese

1. Add the beef, cauliflower, enchilada sauce, chili powder, paprika, garlic powder, black pepper, chilies, and cream cheese to a slow cooker. Stir to mix well. 2. Sprinkle the Cheddar cheese over the top. 3. Cook on low temp setting for 4 to 6 hours or on high for 2 to 3 hours.

Per Serving: Calories 224; Fat 16g; Sodium 822mg; Carbs 0g; Fibre 0g; Sugar 0g; Protein 20g

Hearty Beef Brisket with Sweet Potatoes

Prep time: 15 minutes | Cook time: 8 hours | Serves: 8

1 (1.3kg) beef brisket

1 yellow onion, peeled and diced

Salt and freshly ground black pepper, to taste

2 stalks celery, diced

1 carrot, peeled and diced

1 (300g) box pitted prunes (dried plums)

1 tablespoon dried or freeze-dried parsley

720ml beef stock

3 tablespoons fresh lemon juice

¼ teaspoon ground cloves

1 teaspoon ground cinnamon

1 tablespoon honey

2 tablespoons white or white wine vinegar

4 sweet potatoes, peeled and litreered

1. Add the brisket, onion, salt, pepper, celery, carrot, prunes, and parsley to a slow cooker. 2. In a bowl, mix the stock, lemon juice, cloves, cinnamon, honey, and vinegar and then pour over the meat. Cover the slow cooker and cook on low temp setting for 6 hours or until the meat is cooked through. 3. Add the sweet potatoes. Cover the slow cooker and cook on low temp setting for another 2 hours or until the brisket and sweet potatoes are tender. 4. Use a slotted spoon to move the vegetables and meat to a serving platter. 5. Tent with foil or otherwise cover and keep warm. Allow the meat to rest for 15 minutes before you carve it, slicing it against the grain.

Per Serving: Calories 342; Fat 20g; Sodium 1010mg; Carbs 2g; Fibre 0g; Sugar 0g; Protein 40g

Delicious Pastrami

Prep time: 15 minutes | Cook time: 8¾ hours | Serves: 12

1 (1.7kg) corned beef brisket

2 onions, peeled and sliced

2 cloves of garlic, peeled and minced

2 tablespoons pickling spice

360ml water

1 tablespoon black peppercorns, crushed

¾ teaspoon freshly grated nutmeg

¾ teaspoon ground allspice

2 teaspoons smoked paprika

¼ teaspoon liquid smoke

1. Trim any fat from the corned beef brisket. Add the brisket, onions, garlic, pickling spice, and water to a slow cooker. 2. Cover the slow cooker and cook on low temp setting for 8 hours. Turn off the cooker and allow the meat to cool enough to handle it. 3. Preheat the oven to 175°C. In a bowl, add the crushed peppercorns, nutmeg, allspice, paprika, and liquid smoke and mix well. 4. Rub the peppercorn mixture over all sides of the corned beef. Place beef on a roasting pan; roast on the middle shelf for 45 minutes. 5. Let the meat rest for 10 minutes, then carve by slicing it against the grain or on the diagonal.

Per Serving: Calories 493; Fat 40g; Sodium 857mg; Carbs 1g; Fibre 0g; Sugar 0g; Protein 31g

Swiss Steak and Carrot Stew

Prep time: 15 minutes | Cook time: 8 hours | Serves: 6

65g plain flour

1 teaspoon salt

¼ teaspoon freshly ground black pepper

6 (150g) beef minute steaks

2 tablespoons vegetable oil

2 teaspoons margarine

½ stalk celery, finely diced

1 yellow onion, peeled and diced

240ml beef stock

240ml water

1 (455g) bag baby carrots

Steak sauce, to taste

1. Add the flour, salt, pepper, and minute steaks to a plastic bag; seal and shake to coat the meat. 2. Add the oil and margarine to a frying pan over medium-high heat. After margarine melts and begins to bubble, add the steaks and brown them for 5 minutes on each side (you might have to brown them in batches). 3. Transfer the steaks to a slow cooker. Add the celery to the frying pan and sauté while you add the onion to the plastic bag; seal and shake to coat the onion in flour. 4. Add the flour-coated onions to the frying pan and, stirring constantly, sauté for 10 minutes or until the onions are lightly browned. 5. Add the beef stock to the frying pan and stir to scrape up any browned bits clinging to the pan. Add the water and continue to cook until the liquid is thickened enough to lightly coat the back of a spoon. Pour into the slow cooker. 6. Add the carrots. Cover the slow cooker and cook on low temp setting for 8 hours. Transfer the meat and carrots to a serving platter. Taste the gravy for seasoning, and add steak sauce to taste if desired. 7. Serve gravy alongside or over the meat and carrots.

Per Serving: Calories 356; Fat 24g; Sodium 763mg; Carbs 11g; Fibre 4g; Sugar 2g; Protein 24g

Hot Beef Chili with Corn Chips

Prep time: 15 minutes | Cook time: 6-8 hours | Serves: 4-6

1 tablespoon vegetable oil

1 medium onion, diced

455g lean beef mince

1 (375g) can diced tomatoes, drained

½ red pepper, finely diced

½ green pepper, finely diced

1 tablespoon chili powder

1 teaspoon ground coriander

1 teaspoon ground cumin

1 teaspoon dried oregano

2 teaspoons salt

¼ teaspoon black pepper

Large bag Fritos corn chips, divided

200g grated pareve plain or pepper jack cheese

1. Heat oil in a frying pan over medium-high heat. Add onion and cook, stirring occasionally, for 5–8 minutes or until softened and starting to brown. Transfer to slow cooker and set aside. 2. Add beef mince to frying pan. Break up beef and stir until no pink remains. Drain off grease, then add meat and remaining ingredients except Fritos and cheese to slow cooker. Stir, then cover the slow cooker and cook on low temp setting for 6–8 hours. 3. Crush ¼ Fritos and stir them into chili. Cover and continue to cook another 15 minutes. Place remaining Fritos on serving platter. 4. Ladle chili over Fritos. Top with grated pareve cheese, if desired. Serve immediately.

Per Serving: Calories 396; Fat 28g; Sodium 456mg; Carbs 2g; Fibre 0g; Sugar 0g; Protein 34g

Cheese-Stuffed Meatballs

Prep time: 15 minutes | Cook time: 4-6 hours | Serves: 6

455g 93% lean beef mince

1½ teaspoons Italian seasoning

1 egg

2 tablespoons almond flour

½ teaspoon salt

¼ teaspoon freshly ground black pepper

200g part-skim mozzarella, grated

1 (200g) can low-sodium or no-salt-added diced tomatoes

1. In a bowl, mix the beef, Italian Seasoning, egg, almond flour, salt, and pepper. Using 2 to 4 tablespoons of the meatball mixture, form it into a ball and flatten it. 2. Place 1 to 3 teaspoons of the mozzarella on the centre of the flattened meat. Form the meat around the mozzarella and shape into a ball. Repeat with the remaining meatball mixture and mozzarella. 3. Pour ½ can of the tomatoes into a slow cooker. Add the meatballs. Cover the meatballs with the remaining tomatoes. 4. Cook on low temp setting for 4 to 6 hours or on high for 2 to 3 hours.

Per Serving: Calories 307; Fat 25g; Sodium 633mg; Carbs 7.5g; Fibre 2.5g; Sugar 1g; Protein 13g

Tasty Beef & Mushroom Meatballs

Prep time: 15 minutes | Cook time: 4-6 hours | Serves: 6

1 (200g) can low-sodium or no-salt-added diced tomatoes

100g mushrooms, finely chopped

1 small onion, finely chopped

2 garlic cloves, minced

1 tablespoon Italian Seasoning

½ teaspoon salt

¼ teaspoon freshly ground black pepper

455g 93% lean beef mince

1. Pour the diced tomatoes in the bottom of a slow cooker. 2. In a bowl, combine the mushrooms, onion, garlic, Italian Seasoning, salt, pepper, and beef. Mix until well blended. 3. Form into balls, using 2 to 4 tablespoons of the mixture for each meatball. 4. Add the meatballs to the slow cooker. 5. Cook on low temp setting for 4 to 6 hours or on high for 2 to 3 hours.

Per Serving: Calories 243; Fat 15g; Sodium 632mg; Carbs 2g; Fibre 0.5g; Sugar 0.1g; Protein 25g

Cottage Beef Pie with vegetables

Prep time: 15 minutes | Cook time: 7-9 hours | Serves: 6

1 onion, diced

3 cloves garlic, minced

1 carrot, diced

1 parsnip, diced

1 stalk celery, diced

455g lean beef mince

360ml beef stock

½ teaspoon hot paprika

½ teaspoon crushed rosemary

1 tablespoon Worcestershire sauce

½ teaspoon dried savoury

⅛ teaspoon salt

¼ teaspoon freshly ground black pepper

1 tablespoon cornflour and 1 tablespoon water, mixed (if necessary)

10g minced fresh parsley

630g plain mashed potatoes

1. In a frying pan, sauté the onion, garlic, carrot, parsnip, celery, and beef until the beef mince is browned, about 5 minutes. Drain off any excess fat and discard it. Place the mixture into a round slow cooker. 2. Add the stock, paprika, rosemary, Worcestershire sauce, savoury, salt, and pepper. Stir. Cook on low temp setting for 6–8 hours. 3. If the meat mixture still looks very wet, create a slurry by mixing 1 tablespoon cornflour and 1 tablespoon water. Stir this into the meat mixture. 4. In a bowl, mash the parsley and potatoes using a potato masher. Spread on top of the beef mince mixture in the slow cooker. 5. Cover and cook on high temp setting for 30–60 minutes or until the potatoes are warmed through.

Per Serving: Calories 518; Fat 37g; Sodium 563mg; Carbs 4g; Fibre 0g; Sugar 0g; Protein 36g

Prep time: 15 minutes | Cook time: 8 hours | Serves: 8

2 tablespoons vegetable oil

1 yellow onion, peeled and diced

3 cloves of garlic, peeled and minced

1 (1.3kg) boneless chuck roast, trimmed of fat and cut into 1" cubes

40 g fresh mushrooms, cleaned and sliced

2 tablespoons tomato paste

480ml beef stock or water

960ml burgundy

½ teaspoon thyme

1 bay leaf

Salt and freshly ground black pepper, to taste

1 yellow onion, peeled and thinly sliced

110g margarine, softened

65g plain flour

1. Heat oil in a frying pan over medium-high heat. Add the onion to the frying pan and sauté for 5 minutes or until it is transparent. Stir in the garlic, sauté for 30 seconds, and then transfer the onion mixture to the slow cooker. Cover the cooker. 2. Add the beef cubes to the frying pan and brown the meat over medium-high heat for 5 minutes. Transfer the meat to the slow cooker. Cover the cooker. 3. Add half of the sliced mushrooms to the frying pan; stir-fry for 5 minutes or until the mushroom liquids have evaporated; transfer to the slow cooker and replace the cover. 4. Add the tomato paste to the frying pan and sauté for 3 minutes or until the tomato paste just begins to brown. Stir in the stockor water, scraping the bottom of the pan to remove any browned bits and work them into the sauce. 5. Remove the pan from the heat and stir in the burgundy, thyme, bay leaf, salt, and pepper; stir to combine. Pour into the slow cooker. 6. Add the remaining mushrooms and sliced onions to slow cooker. Cover the slow cooker and cook on low temp setting for 8 hours. 7. To thicken the sauce, use a slotted spoon to transfer the meat, cooked onions, and mushrooms to a serving platter; cover and keep warm. 8. In a bowl, mix the margarine with the flour to form a paste; whisk in some of the pan liquid a little at a time to thin the paste. 9. Strain out any lumps. Increase the heat of the cooker to high. 10. When the pan liquids begin to bubble around the edges, whisk in the flour mixture. Cook, stirring constantly, for 15 minutes or until the sauce has thickened enough to coat the back of a spoon. 11. Pour over the meat, mushrooms, and onions on the serving platter.

Per Serving: Calories 384; Fat 28g; Sodium 941mg; Carbs 2g; Fibre 0g; Sugar 0g; Protein 34g

Chapter 6 Soup, Chili and Stew

Peppercorn Vegetable Stock

Prep time: 5 minutes | Cook time: 10 hours | Serves: 6

4 celery ribs, ends trimmed but leaves intact, cut into 4 pieces

4 medium carrots, washed, ends trimmed, cut into 4 pieces

1 yellow onion, litreered

4 garlic cloves, peeled and left whole

2 bay leaves

½ teaspoon whole peppercorns

9L water

Parsley, thyme, and/or rosemary sprigs

1. In a slow cooker, combine the celery, carrots, onion, garlic, bay leaves, peppercorns, water, and herbs. 2. Cover the slow cooker and cook on low temp setting for 10 hours, until the flavours have melded. 3. Cool the stockto room temperature, then strain through a fine-mesh strainer lined with cheesecloth. Discard the solids.

Per Serving: Calories 285; Fat 16g; Sodium 497mg; Carbs 1g; Fibre 0g; Sugar 1g; Protein 34g

Bacon and Beans Chili

Prep time: 15 minutes | Cook time: 8 hours | Serves: 6

455g dried pinto beans, rinsed and picked over

1 tablespoon plus salt, ½ teaspoon, divided

960ml water

2 (200g) cans tomato sauce

2 tablespoons molasses

1 tablespoon Dijon mustard

Freshly ground black pepper

5 slices cooked bacon, crumbled

1. The night before you make the soup, put the beans in a large bowl and add enough water to cover them by 5cm. Sprinkle in 1 tablespoon of salt. Soak the beans for at least 8 hours. Rinse the beans thoroughly. Put the beans in the slow cooker. Add 960ml fresh water. 2. Cover the slow cooker and cook on low temp setting for 8 hours until the beans are tender. 3. Drain off any extra water. Add the tomato sauce, molasses, mustard, remaining ½ teaspoon of salt, and a few grinds of pepper and stir. 4. Add the crumbled bacon and serve.

Per Serving: Calories 101; Fat 5g; Sodium 214mg; Carbs 6g; Fibre 0g; Sugar 0g; Protein 11g

Beef and Kidney Beans Chili with Spaghetti

Prep time: 15 minutes | Cook time: 8 hours | Serves: 4-6

195g dried kidney beans, rinsed and picked over

3 teaspoons salt, divided

600ml water

455g lean beef mince

1 tablespoon chili powder

1 teaspoon ground cumin

1 teaspoon ground cinnamon

½ teaspoon garlic powder

½ teaspoon onion powder

¼ teaspoon freshly ground black pepper, plus more for seasoning

2 (200g) cans tomato sauce

Cooked spaghetti, for serving

100g grated Cheddar cheese, for garnish

110g chopped red onion, for garnish

1. The night before you make the chili, put the dried beans in a large bowl and add enough water to cover them by 5cm. Sprinkle in 2 teaspoons of salt. Soak the beans for at least 8 hours. Rinse the beans thoroughly. Put the beans in the slow cooker. Pour in 600ml fresh water. 2. Add the beef mince, chili powder, cumin, cinnamon, garlic powder, onion powder, remaining 1 teaspoon of salt, and the pepper and stir to combine. 3. Cover the slow cooker and cook on low temp setting for 8 hours until the beans are tender. 4. Stir in the tomato sauce: Season with salt and pepper, if desired. 5. To serve, pile some spaghetti on each plate and ladle the chili over the top. 6. Garnish with Cheddar cheese and chopped red onion, if desired.

Per Serving: Calories 111; Fat 9g; Sodium 632mg; Carbs 5g; Fibre 1g; Sugar 1g; Protein 4g

Chicken & Courgette Soup

Prep time: 10 minutes | Cook time: 4-6 hours | Serves: 4

455g boneless, skinless chicken thighs

1.4L low-sodium chicken stock

2 medium courgette, cut into spaghetti-like strands

2 celery stalks, sliced

2 carrots, peeled and chopped

2 garlic cloves, minced

1 teaspoon cumin

½ teaspoon salt

¼ teaspoon freshly ground black pepper

1. Add the chicken, stock, courgette, celery, carrots, garlic, cumin, salt, and pepper to the slow cooker. Stir to mix well. 2. Cook on low temp setting for 4 to 6 hours or on high for 2 to 3 hours. 3. Remove the chicken from the slow cooker, shred it, toss it back into the soup, and serve.

Per Serving: Calories 237; Fat 15g; Sodium 469mg; Carbs 2g; Fibre 1g; Sugar 1g; Protein 22g

Chili con Carne

Prep time: 15 minutes | Cook time: 8 hours | Serves: 4

455g beef chuck roast, trimmed of fat and cut into bite-size pieces

1½ teaspoons chili powder

1 teaspoon ground cumin

1 teaspoon garlic powder

½ teaspoon salt, plus more for Seasoning

¼ teaspoon freshly ground black pepper, plus more

for seasoning

1 medium yellow onion, finely diced

2 (360g) cans petite diced tomatoes

2 tablespoons tomato paste

180ml water

1 (375g) can kidney beans, rinsed and drained

1. Put the beef in the slow cooker. Sprinkle on the chili powder, cumin, garlic powder, salt, and pepper. Stir to combine. 2. Add the onion, tomatoes with their juice, tomato paste, water, and beans. Stir to combine. 3. Cover the slow cooker and cook on low temp setting for 8 hours until the beef is tender. 4. Stir the chili and spice with salt and pepper, if desired. Ladle into bowls and serve.

Per Serving: Calories 331; Fat 24g; Sodium 943mg; Carbs 8g; Fibre 3g; Sugar 5g; Protein 18g

Basil Chicken Orzo Soup

Prep time: 15 minutes | Cook time: 7-8 hours | Serves: 6

455g boneless, skinless chicken breasts

960ml Savoury Vegetable Stock

480ml Chicken Stock

2 carrots, sliced

2 celery stalks, finely chopped

6 garlic cloves, minced

1 teaspoon dried basil

1 teaspoon Italian seasoning

2 bay leaves

Juice of 1 lemon

15g chopped fresh parsley

200g orzo

Freshly ground black pepper

1. Place the chicken, vegetable stock, chicken stock, carrots, celery, garlic, basil, Italian seasoning, and bay leaves in a slow cooker. Cover the slow cooker and cook on low temp setting for 7 to 8 hours. 2. About 30 minutes prior to serving, remove and discard the bay leaves. Use two forks to shred the chicken. Stir in the lemon juice, parsley, orzo, and pepper. Cook for 30 minutes, until the orzo is tender, stirring every 10 minutes to prevent sticking. 3. Serve immediately.

Per Serving: Calories 289; Fat 19g; Sodium 1244mg; Carbs 9g; Fibre 1g; Sugar 3g; Protein 17g

Spicy Black Bean Soup

Prep time: 10 minutes | Cook time: 8-10 hours | Serves: 6

455g dried black beans

2 (350g) cans no-salt-added diced tomatoes

720ml Savoury Vegetable Stock

½ red onion, diced

1 green pepper, seeded and diced

1 poblano pepper, seeded and diced

2 jalapeño peppers, seeded and diced

3 tablespoons red wine vinegar

6 garlic cloves, minced

1½ tablespoons chili powder

2 teaspoons ground cumin

½ teaspoon dried oregano

½ teaspoon salt

½ teaspoon freshly ground black pepper

2 bay leaves

1. Soak the beans overnight at room temperature in a bowl with 2 litres of water. 2. Drain and rinse the beans and put them in a slow cooker. Add the tomatoes, stock, onion, pepper, poblano, jalapeños, vinegar, garlic, chili powder, cumin, oregano, salt, pepper, and bay leaves and stir well. Cover and cook on high temp setting for 8 to 10 hours. 3. Remove the bay leaves before serving. Stir and serve hot.

Per Serving: Calories 169; Fat 13g; Sodium 965mg; Carbs 9g; Fibre 3g; Sugar 5g; Protein 3g

Navy Bean Soup and Ham Soup

Prep time: 10 minutes | Cook time: 8-10 hours | Serves: 8

455g dried navy beans

480ml Chicken Stock

1 (375g) can no-salt-added diced tomatoes

200g 98% fat-free, reduced-sodium ham, finely diced

3 celery ribs, diced

3 carrots, diced

1 onion, diced

3 garlic cloves, minced

1½ teaspoons onion powder

1 teaspoon dried parsley

1 teaspoon dried sage

1 teaspoon garlic powder

1 bay leaf

½ teaspoon freshly ground black pepper

½ teaspoon salt

1. Rinse the beans and put them in a slow cooker. Cover the beans with about 2.5cm of water and add the rest of the ingredients. Stir well. 2. Cover the slow cooker and cook on low temp setting for 8 to 10 hours. 3. Use the back of a spoon to mash some of the beans against the sides of the slow cooker and stir them back into the soup, creating a creamier texture. 4. Serve hot.

Per Serving: Calories 568; Fat 45g; Sodium 968mg; Carbs 5g; Fibre 1g; Sugar 2g; Protein 27g

Creamy Sweet Potato Soup

Prep time: 15 minutes | Cook time: 7-8 hours | Serves: 6

4 medium sweet potatoes, sliced

960ml Savoury Vegetable Stock

480ml unsweetened almond milk or low-fat milk

2 medium carrots, chopped

1 onion, sliced

1 tablespoon minced garlic

1 tablespoon minced fresh ginger

2 teaspoons ground cumin

⅛ teaspoon ground nutmeg

Freshly ground black pepper

1. Combine all the ingredients in a slow cooker. Cover the slow cooker and cook on low temp setting for 7 to 8 hours. 2. Using a blender or standing blender, blend the soup until smooth. 3. Serve warm.

Per Serving: Calories 602; Fat 45g; Sodium 689mg; Carbs 2g; Fibre 0g; Sugar 0g; Protein 46g

Mixed Beans and Barely Soup

Prep time: 15 minutes | Cook time: 7-8 hours | Serves: 6-8

1.4 L savoury vegetable stock

1 (200g) can no-salt-added diced tomatoes

1 (360g) can white kidney beans, drained and rinsed

1 (360g) can red kidney beans, drained and rinsed

2 onions, chopped

3 celery stalks, chopped

2 carrots, chopped

1 medium courgette, diced

150g fresh green beans, trimmed and cut into 1cm pieces

30g chopped fresh spinach

90g hulled barley

4 garlic cloves, minced

1 tablespoon chopped fresh parsley

Freshly ground black pepper

1. Combine all the ingredients in a slow cooker. Cover the slow cooker and cook on low temp setting for 7 to 8 hours. 2. Serve warm.

Per Serving: Calories 107; Fat 6g; Sodium 423mg; Carbs 6g; Fibre 1g; Sugar 2g; Protein 8g

Cheesy Beef and Courgette Soup

Prep time: 20 minutes | Cook time: 6 hours | Serves: 6

3 tablespoons extra-virgin olive oil, divided

455g beef mince

½ sweet onion, chopped

2 teaspoons minced garlic

960ml beef stock

1 (200g) can diced tomatoes, undrained

1 courgette, diced

1½ tablespoons dried basil

2 teaspoons dried oregano

100g cream cheese

120g grated mozzarella

1. Lightly grease the slow cooker with 1 tablespoon of the olive oil. 2. In a frying pan over medium-high heat, heat the remaining 2 tablespoons of the olive oil. add the beef mince and sauté until it is cooked through, about 6 minutes. 3. Add the onion and garlic and sauté for 3 minutes. 4. Transfer the meat mixture to the slow cooker. 5. Stir in the stock, tomatoes, courgette, basil, and oregano. 6. Cover the slow cooker and cook on low temp setting for 6 hours. 7. Stir in the cream cheese and mozzarella and serve.

Per Serving: Calories 270; Fat 14g; Sodium 426mg; Carbs 6g; Fibre 2g; Sugar 1g; Protein 29g

Creamy Chicken and Bacon Soup

Prep time: 15 minutes | Cook time: 8 hours | Serves: 8

1 tablespoon extra-virgin olive oil

1.4L chicken stock

420g cooked chicken, chopped

1 sweet onion, chopped

2 celery stalks, chopped

1 carrot, diced

2 teaspoons minced garlic

360g double cream

240g cream cheese

80g cooked chopped bacon

1 tablespoon chopped fresh parsley, for garnish

1. Lightly grease the slow cooker with the olive oil. 2. Add the stock, chicken, onion, celery, carrot, and garlic. 3. Cover the slow cooker and cook on low temp setting for 8 hours. 4. Stir in the double cream, cream cheese, and bacon. 5. serve topped with the parsley.

Per Serving: Calories 129; Fat 9g; Sodium 236mg; Carbs 6g; Fibre 2g; Sugar 2g; Protein 7g

Sausage and Kale Soup

Prep time: 15 minutes | Cook time: 6 hours | Serves: 6

3 tablespoons olive oil, divided

675g sausage, without casing

1.4L chicken stock

2 celery stalks, chopped

1 carrot, diced

1 leek, thoroughly cleaned and chopped

2 teaspoons minced garlic

60g chopped kale

1 tablespoon chopped fresh parsley, for garnish

1. Lightly grease the slow cooker with 1 tablespoon of the olive oil. 2. In a frying pan over medium-high heat, heat the remaining 2 tablespoons of the olive oil. add the sausage and sauté until it is cooked through, about 7 minutes. 3. Transfer the sausage to the slow cooker, and stir in the stock, celery, carrot, leek, and garlic. 4. Cover the slow cooker and cook on low temp setting for 6 hours. 5. Stir in the kale. Serve topped with the parsley.

Per Serving: Calories 175; Fat 14g; Sodium 265mg; Carbs 4g; Fibre 1g; Sugar 2g; Protein 9g

Creamy Beef Soup

Prep time: 15 minutes | Cook time: 6 hours | Serves: 8

3 tablespoons olive oil, divided

455g beef mince

1 sweet onion, chopped

2 teaspoons minced garlic

1.4L beef stock

1 (200g) can diced tomatoes

2 celery stalks, chopped

1 carrot, chopped

240g heavy cream

200g grated cheddar cheese

½ teaspoon freshly ground black pepper

1 spring onion, white and green parts, chopped, for garnish

1. Lightly grease the slow cooker with 1 tablespoon of the olive oil. 2. In a frying pan over medium-high heat, heat the remaining 2 tablespoons of the olive oil. add the beef mince and sauté until it is cooked through, about 6 minutes. 3. Add the onion and garlic and sauté for 3 minutes. 4. Transfer the beef mixture to the slow cooker, and stir in the stock, tomatoes, celery, and carrot. 5. Cover the slow cooker and cook on low temp setting for 6 hours. 6. Stir in the double cream, cheese, and pepper. 7. Serve hot, topped with the spring onion.

Per Serving: Calories 215; Fat 11g; Sodium 135mg; Carbs 3g; Fibre 1g; Sugar 1g; Protein 27g

Creamy Chicken and Mushroom Soup

Prep time: 15 minutes | Cook time: 6 hours | Serves: 6

1 tablespoon coconut oil

250g boneless, skinless chicken thighs, cut into

2.5cm chunks

Salt

Freshly ground black pepper

2 tablespoons unsalted butter

2 celery stalks, diced ½ onion, diced

3 garlic cloves, minced

200g cremini mushrooms, thinly sliced

960ml chicken stock, divided

½ teaspoon dried thyme

1 bay leaf

240g double cream

2 tablespoons chopped fresh flat-leaf parsley

1. In a frying pan, heat the coconut oil over medium-high heat. 2. Season the chicken with salt and pepper and add it to the frying pan. Sauté until browned on all sides, about 5 minutes. Transfer the chicken to the slow cooker. 3. Return the frying pan to medium-high heat and add the butter. When it has melted, add the celery, onion, garlic, and mushrooms and sauté until softened, about 5 minutes. 4. Add 240ml of chicken stock to the frying pan to deglaze it. Bring to a boil and cook for about 1 minute, stirring and scraping up any browned bits from the bottom. Carefully pour the mixture into the slow cooker. 5. Stir the remaining 720ml of stock, thyme, and bay leaf into the cooker. Cover and cook for 6 hours on low temp setting. 6. Just before serving, stir in the double cream and parsley. Serve hot.

Per Serving: Calories 248; Fat 24g; Sodium 170mg; Carbs 9g; Fibre 5g; Sugar 1g; Protein 3g

Tangy Beef Bone Stock

Prep time: 15 minutes | Cook time: 12-24 hours | Serves: 4-6

1.7kg beef bones

1 onion, roughly chopped

6 garlic cloves, peeled and smashed with the flat

side of a knife

2 bay leaves

60ml apple cider vinegar

1 tablespoon salt

4 litres cold water

1. In the slow cooker, combine the beef bones, onion, garlic, bay leaves, cider vinegar, and salt. 2. Pour in the water, Cover and cook for at least 12 hours, and as long as 24 hours, on low. When finished, let cool. 3. Strain the stock through a fine-mesh sieve and discard the solids.

Per Serving: Calories 289; Fat 26g; Sodium 147mg; Carbs 10g; Fibre 7g; Sugar 2g; Protein 6g

Coconut Curry Chicken Soup

Prep time: 10 minutes | Cook time: 6 hours | Serves: 6

2 (350g) cans coconut milk

480ml chicken stock

65g all-natural peanut butter

2 tablespoons red curry paste, or more for Seasoning

2 tablespoons fish sauce

675g boneless, skinless chicken thighs, cut into

2.5cm pieces

1 red pepper, seeded and cut into ½cm-wide slices

1 small onion, thinly sliced

1 tablespoon minced fresh ginger

1 tablespoon freshly squeezed lime juice

10g chopped fresh coriander

1. In the slow cooker, stir the coconut milk, chicken stock, peanut butter, curry paste, and fish sauce. 2. Add the chicken, red pepper, onion, and ginger. Cover and cook for 6 hours on low temp setting. 3. Just before serving, stir in the lime juice and garnish with the coriander. Serve hot.

Per Serving: Calories 233; Fat 23g; Sodium 111mg; Carbs 6g; Fibre 1g; Sugar 0.6g; Protein 3g

Coconut Chicken Curry with Cauliflower & Spinach

Prep time: 10 minutes | Cook time: 6 hours | Serves: 6

1.4L chicken stock

480ml canned coconut milk

180g coconut cream

3 tablespoons curry powder

2 tablespoons erythritol

1 teaspoon salt

200g boneless, skinless chicken thighs, diced

125g riced cauliflower

90g baby spinach

1. In the slow cooker, combine the chicken stock, coconut milk, coconut cream, curry powder, erythritol, salt, chicken, and cauliflower. Cover and cook for 6 hours on low temp setting. 2. Just before serving, stir in the spinach until it is wilted. Serve hot.

Per Serving: Calories 101; Fat 5g; Sodium 214mg; Carbs 6g; Fibre 0g; Sugar 0g; Protein 11g

Warm Vegetable Stock

Prep time: 5 minutes | Cook time: 8-12 hours | Serves: 12

1 tablespoon extra-virgin olive oil

3 onions, litreered

3 celery stalks, cut into 8cm pieces

6 garlic cloves, peeled and smashed with the flat side of a knife

1 bay leaf

1 tablespoon salt

½ teaspoon black peppercorns

4 litres water

1. In the slow cooker, combine the olive oil, onions, celery, garlic, bay leaf, salt, and peppercorns. 2. Pour in the water. Cover and cook for 8 to 12 hours on low temp setting. When finished, let cool. 3. Strain the stockthrough a fine-mesh sieve and discard the solids.

Per Serving: Calories 111; Fat 9g; Sodium 632mg; Carbs 5g; Fibre 1g; Sugar 1g; Protein 4g

Beef and Cabbage Soup

Prep time: 20 minutes | Cook time: 8-10 hours | Serves: 6

2 tablespoons coconut oil

200g beef stew meat, diced

Salt

Freshly ground black pepper

200g smoked beef sausage, diced

1 onion, finely chopped

210g grated cabbage

480ml beef stock

1 (375g) can tomato sauce

2 garlic cloves, minced

2 bay leaves

3 tablespoons chopped fresh parsley

240g sour cream

1. In a frying pan, heat the coconut oil over medium-high heat. 2. Generously spice the meat with salt and pepper and add it to the frying pan, along with the sausage. Cook until the meat is browned on all sides, about 6 minutes. Transfer the beef and sausage to the slow cooker. 3. Return the frying pan to medium-high heat and add the onion. Sauté until softened, about 4 minutes. Transfer the onion to the slow cooker. 4. Add the cabbage, beef stock, tomato sauce, garlic, and bay leaves to the slow cooker. Cover and cook for 8 to 10 hours on low temp setting. 5. Serve hot, garnished with the parsley and a dollop of sour cream.

Per Serving: Calories 319; Fat 22g; Sodium 430mg; Carbs 1g; Fibre 0g; Sugar 0g; Protein 29g

Chicken Rice Soup

Prep time: 15 minutes | Cook time: 7-9 hours | Serves: 8

2 litres chicken stock

2 carrots, peeled and diced

2 stalks celery, diced

5cm piece of fresh ginger, peeled and minced (or 2 teaspoons ground ginger)

1 lime, juiced (about 2 tablespoons)

1 onion, peeled and finely diced

4 cloves garlic, minced

½ teaspoon salt

½ teaspoon freshly ground pepper

15g minced coriander

300g cooked rice, any variety

280g diced cooked chicken

1. Place the stock, carrots, celery, ginger, lime juice, onion, garlic, salt, and pepper in a slow cooker. Stir. 2. Cook on low temp setting for 7–9 hours. Stir in the coriander, rice, and chicken. Cook on high for 15–30 minutes. Stir prior to serving.

Per Serving: Calories 164; Fat 8g; Sodium 397mg; Carbs 5g; Fibre 0g; Sugar 0g; Protein 16g

Delicious Chicken Congee

Prep time: 15 minutes | Cook time: 2-3 hours | Serves: 4

960ml chicken stock

240ml water

90g uncooked long grain rice

1 teaspoon ground ginger

1 cooked chicken breast, grated or thinly sliced

2 teaspoons soy sauce (or more to taste)

3 spring onions, green parts thinly sliced or chopped

1. Combine chicken stock, water, rice, and ground ginger in a slow cooker. Cover and cook on high temp setting for 2–3 hours or until rice breaks up and soup thickens. 2. Uncover and add chicken. Re-cover and continue to heat for another 30 minutes. Uncover and stir in soy sauce. 3. Taste and add more soy sauce if needed. Ladle soup into bowls. Garnish with spring onion s. Serve hot.

Per Serving: Calories 318; Fat 19g; Sodium 546mg; Carbs 4g; Fibre 0g; Sugar 2g; Protein 28g

Buffalo Cheese Chicken Chili

Prep time: 10 minutes | Cook time: 6 hours | Serves: 6

675g boneless, skinless chicken thighs, trimmed of excess fat

2 (375g) cans great northern beans, rinsed and drained

1 (360g) can diced fire-roasted tomatoes

480ml chicken stock

60 – 120g buffalo wing sauce

½ teaspoon onion powder

½ teaspoon garlic powder

¼ teaspoon salt

200g cream cheese

Blue cheese crumbles

1. Combine the chicken, beans, tomatoes with their juice, stock, 60g of buffalo wing sauce, onion powder, garlic powder, and salt in the slow cooker. 2. Cover the slow cooker and cook on low temp setting for 6 hours. 3. Cut the cream cheese into cubes and stir them into the slow cooker. Transfer the chicken to a cutting board. Shred the chicken with two forks or cut it into small pieces. Return the chicken to the slow cooker. 4. When the cream cheese is melted and incorporated into the chili, ladle the chili into bowls and serve. Top with blue cheese crumbles, if desired.

Per Serving: Calories 233; Fat 23g; Sodium 111mg; Carbs 6g; Fibre 1g; Sugar 0.6g; Protein 3g

Easy Pho Soup

Prep time: 15 minutes | Cook time: 4 hours | Serves: 6

1 tablespoon coriander seeds

1 tablespoon whole cloves

6 star anise

1 cinnamon stick

1 tablespoon fennel seed

1 tablespoon whole cardamom

10cm section of fresh ginger, peeled and sliced

1 onion, sliced

1.9L no-beef stock

1 teaspoon soy sauce

200g rice noodles

1 cooked chicken breast, thinly sliced or grated

15g chopped coriander

15g chopped Thai basil

260g mung bean sprouts

30g sliced spring onion s

1. In a dry frying pan, quickly heat the spices, ginger, and onion until the seeds start to pop, about 5 minutes. The onion and ginger should look slightly caramelized. 2. Place the mixture in a cheesecloth packet and tie it securely with food-safe twine. 3. In a slow cooker, place the cheesecloth packet. Add the stock, soy sauce, noodles, and chicken. Cover the slow cooker and cook on low temp setting for 4 hours. 4. Remove the cheesecloth packet after cooking. Ladle soup into bowls. Top with coriander, basil, sprouts, and spring onions.

Per Serving: Calories 344; Fat 16g; Sodium 711mg; Carbs 41.56g; Fibre 2.6g; Sugar 1.94g; Protein 13.29g

Creamy Mushroom Soup

Prep time: 15 minutes | Cook time: 4-6 hours | Serves: 6

455g mixed wild mushrooms, sliced, divided

55g unsalted butter

1 medium onion, peeled and diced

2 garlic cloves, minced

480ml vegetable stock

480ml water

2 teaspoons fresh thyme leaves

1 bay leaf

240ml dry sherry

1 (375g) can evaporated milk

1 teaspoon salt

¼ teaspoon ground black pepper

15g minced fresh parsley leaves, chopped

2 tablespoons chopped chives

1. Coarsely chop 25g of the sliced mushrooms and set aside. 2. Melt the butter in a frying pan over medium-high heat. Add the diced onion and cook, stirring occasionally, until onions soften and start to brown, about 5–8 minutes. 3. Add garlic and stir for one minute. Add remaining sliced mushrooms and cook for 5 more minutes, or just until mushrooms start to reduce and give off their liquid. 4. Transfer sautéed vegetables to a slow cooker. Add in the vegetable stock, water, thyme, and bay leaf. 5. Cover the slow cooker and cook on low temp setting for 4–6 hours. Remove. Stir in the sherry and evaporated milk. Set the cover ajar and cook for 15 minutes to allow alcohol to evaporate. 6. Add the salt and black pepper. Taste and add salt and/or pepper if needed. 7. Ladle into bowls and garnish with the chopped parsley leaves, chives, and the coarsely chopped mushrooms.

Per Serving: Calories 255; Fat 10g; Sodium 475mg; Carbs 2g; Fibre 1g; Sugar 0g; Protein 34g

Creamed Corn and Potato Soup

Prep time: 15 minutes | Cook time: 6 hours | Serves: 4

55g margarine

1 onion, diced

1 jalapeño, minced

150g diced tomato

2 medium russet potatoes, peeled and diced

2 (375g) cans creamed corn

480ml water

480ml unsweetened soy milk or rice milk

1 teaspoon chili powder

1 teaspoon cumin

¼ teaspoon cayenne pepper

Salt and pepper, to taste

1. In a sauté pan over medium heat, melt the margarine; add the onion and jalapeño, and sauté for about 3 minutes. 2. In a slow cooker, add all ingredients. Cover the slow cooker and cook on low temp setting heat for 6 hours.

Per Serving: Calories 185; Fat 7g; Sodium 731mg; Carbs 1g; Fibre 0g; Sugar 0g; Protein 27g

Colourful Garden Vegetable Soup

Prep time: 10 minutes | Cook time: 6-8 hours | Serves: 4

960ml stock

1 (375g) can low-sodium or no-salt-added diced tomatoes

2 small courgettes, diced

2 carrots, peeled and chopped

100g green beans, chopped

100g kale, chopped

1 onion, diced

1 pepper, seeded and diced

2 garlic cloves, minced

1 tablespoon Italian seasoning

½ teaspoon salt

¼ teaspoon freshly ground black pepper

1 bay leaf

1. Add the stock, tomatoes, courgette, carrots, green beans, kale, onion, pepper, garlic, Italian seasoning, salt, black pepper, and bay leaf to a slow cooker. 2. Cook on low temp setting for 6 to 8 hours or on high for 3 to 4 hours until vegetables are soft. 3. Remove the bay leaf prior to serving.

Per Serving: Calories 432; Fat 22g; Sodium 623mg; Carbs 1g; Fibre 0g; Sugar 0g; Protein 48g

Classic French Onion Soup

Prep time: 10 minutes | Cook time: 6-8 hours | Serves: 4

960ml low-sodium beef stock

4 medium white onions, sliced as thin as possible

2 tablespoons unsalted butter

2 garlic cloves, minced

½ teaspoon salt

¼ teaspoon freshly ground black pepper

1 bay leaf

4 (25g) slices provolone cheese

1. Add the stock, onions, butter, garlic, bay leaf, salt and pepper to a slow cooker. Stir to mix well. 2. Cook on low temp setting for 6 to 8 hours or on high for 3 to 4 hours. 3. Preheat the oven to grill. 4. Ladle the soup into 4 oven-safe soup bowls and place on a baking sheet. Place 1 slice of provolone over the soup in each bowl, and grill for 1 minute until the cheese melts.

Per Serving: Calories 533; Fat 30g; Sodium 845mg; Carbs 3g; Fibre 0g; Sugar 0g; Protein 52g

Delicious Chicken Fajita Soup

Prep time: 10 minutes | Cook time: 6-8 hours | Serves: 4

900g boneless, skinless chicken thighs

2 peppers, seeded and sliced

1 onion, sliced

1 (200g) can low-sodium or no-salt-added diced tomatoes

2 teaspoons chili powder

1 teaspoon ground cumin

½ teaspoon paprika

½ teaspoon salt

½ teaspoon freshly ground black pepper

⅛ teaspoon garlic powder

⅛ teaspoon onion powder

⅛ teaspoon oregano

⅛ teaspoon red pepper flakes

1. Add the chicken, peppers, onion, tomatoes, chili powder, cumin, paprika, salt, black pepper, oregano, garlic powder, onion powder, and red pepper flakes to a slow cooker. Stir to mix well. 2. Cook on low temp setting for 6 to 8 hours or on high for 3 to 4 hours.

Per Serving: Calories 156; Fat 7g; Sodium 404mg; Carbs 1g; Fibre 0g; Sugar 0g; Protein 21g

Lime Chicken Avocado Soup

Prep time: 5 minutes | Cook time: 4-6 hours | Serves: 6

455g bone-in chicken breast

1.9L low-sodium chicken stock

2 spring onions (whites and greens), sliced

1 tomato, diced

1 celery stalk, sliced

2 garlic cloves, minced

¼ teaspoon cumin

1 teaspoon salt

1 teaspoon freshly ground black pepper

1 tablespoon freshly squeezed lime juice

10g chopped fresh coriander, plus whole coriander leaves for garnish

2 avocados, sliced

Lime wedges, for garnish

1. Add the chicken, stock, spring onions, tomato, celery, garlic, cumin, salt, pepper, lime juice, and coriander to a slow cooker. 2. Cook on low temp setting for 4 to 6 hours or on high for 2 to 3 hours. 3. Remove the chicken, shred the meat from the bones, and add the grated meat back into the slow cooker. Stir to combine. 4. Ladle into 6 bowls and top with avocado slices. 5. Serve with lime wedges on the side.

Per Serving: Calories 416; Fat 26g; Sodium 666mg; Carbs 0g; Fibre 0g; Sugar 0g; Protein 36g

Japanese Triple Pork Soup

Prep time: 20 minutes | Cook time: 8 hours | Serves: 6-8

300g boneless pork shoulder, trimmed of excess fat and cut into 2 or 3 pieces

1 teaspoon salt

2 tablespoons coconut oil

100g pork belly

4 bacon slices, chopped

1 onion, diced

6 garlic cloves, minced

1 (5cm) piece fresh ginger, peeled and minced

1.7L chicken stock, divided

200g cremini or button mushrooms, sliced

1 leek (white and pale green parts), halved lengthwise and thinly sliced crosswise

1 tablespoon soy sauce or tamari

¼ head napa cabbage, thinly sliced, divided

100g bean sprouts, divided

1 tablespoon toasted sesame oil

1. Season the pork shoulder with the salt. 2. In a frying pan, heat the coconut oil over medium-high heat. Add the pork shoulder, pork belly, and bacon. Cook until browned on all sides, about 8 minutes. Transfer the meat to the slow cooker. 3. Return the frying pan to medium-high heat and add the onion. Sauté until softened, about 3 minutes. 4. Stir the garlic, ginger, and 240ml of chicken stock into the frying pan. Cook for 1 minute, stirring and scraping up any browned bits from the bottom of the pan. Transfer the mixture to the slow cooker. 5. Add the mushrooms, leek, and remaining of chicken stock to the cooker. Cover and cook for 8 hours on low temp setting. 6. Transfer the pork shoulder to a bowl. Using two forks, shred the meat. Stir the grated meat back into the stock, along with the soy sauce. 7. To serve, fill each serving bowl with a handful each of cabbage and bean sprouts. Ladle the soup, including the meat and vegetables, over the cabbage and bean sprouts. Drizzle a bit of sesame oil over the top and serve hot.

Per Serving: Calories 316; Fat 22g; Sodium 720mg; Carbs 27.8g; Fibre 0g; Sugar 2.27g; Protein 29g

Spicy Mushroom and Tofu Soup

Prep time: 15 minutes | Cook time: 6 hours | Serves: 6

960ml vegetable stock

2 tablespoons soy sauce

2 tablespoons rice vinegar

1 teaspoon sesame oil

50g dried Chinese mushrooms

65g canned bamboo shoots, sliced

100g extra-firm tofu, cubed

1 tablespoon red chili paste

1 teaspoon white pepper

2 tablespoons cornflour mixed with 60ml cold water

1.In a slow cooker, add all ingredients except for the cornflour mixture; cook on low for 6 hours. 2. Pour in the cornflour mixture; stir, and cook on high temp setting for 20 minutes.

Per Serving: Calories 364; Fat 16g; Sodium 415mg; Carbs 3g; Fibre 1g; Sugar 1g; Protein 43g

Tangy Chocolate Fondue

Prep time: 5 minutes | Cook time: 30 minutes | Serves: 6

150g semisweet chocolate

120g double cream

Suggested dipping treats: pretzels, banana slices,

angel food cake squares, strawberries, graham crackers, marshmallows, dried pineapple rounds

1. Break up the chocolate into small pieces and put them in the slow cooker. Pour the cream over the chocolate. 2. Cover and cook on high temp setting for 30 minutes. Stir. 3. If melted, then turn the slow cooker to warm. If it's not melted, then cook on high temp setting for a few more minutes until it is. Dip favourite treats in the chocolate.

Per Serving: Calories 136; Fat 12g; Sodium 33mg; Carbs 8g; Fibre 2g; Sugar 1g; Protein 2g

Baked Apples

Prep time: 15 minutes | Cook time: 4-5 hours | Serves: 6

6 apples

80g rolled oats

40g chopped almonds

2 tablespoons brown sugar

2 teaspoons pumpkin pie spice

120ml apple juice

2 tablespoons extra-virgin olive oil

1. Core the apples using an apple corer or sharp knife. Chop off the top of the apple along with its stem so that the top of the apple is even. 2. In a bowl, combine the oats, almonds, brown sugar, and pumpkin pie spice. 3. Stuff the apple cavities with the oat mixture, pressing the mixture down firmly to pack it in. Top off the apples with any remaining oat mixture. 4. Pour the apple juice into a slow cooker and carefully add the apples so they are standing upright. Drizzle the apples with the olive oil. Cover the slow cooker and cook on low temp setting for 4 to 5 hours, until the apples are tender. 5. Remove the apples from the slow cooker and allow to cool for 5 to 10 minutes before serving.

Per Serving: Calories 297; Fat 25g; Sodium 143mg; Carbs 12g; Fibre 5g; Sugar 2g; Protein 8g

Warm Vanilla Pear Crisp

Prep time: 10 minutes | Cook time: 4-5 hours | Serves: 6

5 pears, chopped (peeling is optional)

1 apple, chopped (peeling is optional)

75g finely chopped dried figs

75g loosely packed brown sugar

2 teaspoons ground cinnamon

2 teaspoons vanilla extract

1 teaspoon ground nutmeg

65g whole-wheat flour, divided

80g old-fashioned oats

70g honey

2 tablespoons coconut oil

1. Put the pears, apple, and figs in a slow cooker. 2. In a bowl, combine the brown sugar, cinnamon, vanilla, nutmeg, and 30g of flour. Pour this over the fruit and stir to combine. 3. In the same bowl, combine the oats, remaining flour, honey, and coconut oil. Spread this mixture on top of the fruit. 4. Cover the slow cooker and cook on low temp setting for 4 to 5 hours, until the fruit is soft. 5. Serve warm.

Per Serving: Calories 304; Fat 24g; Sodium 247mg; Carbs 20g; Fibre 7g; Sugar 6g; Protein 15g

Traditional Blackberry Cobbler

Prep time: 15 minutes | Cook time: 3-4 hours | Serves: 10

For the Filling

1 tablespoon coconut oil

865g blackberries

For the Topping

190g ground almonds

15g granulated erythritol

1 tablespoon baking powder

10g granulated erythritol

1 teaspoon ground cinnamon

½ teaspoon salt

240g double cream

110g butter, melted

1. Lightly grease a slow cooker with the coconut oil. 2. Add the blackberries, erythritol, and cinnamon to the slow cooker. Mix to combine. 3. In a bowl, stir the almonds, erythritol, baking powder, and salt. Add the double cream and butter and stir until a thick batter forms. 4. Drop the batter by the tablespoon on top of the blackberries.5. Cover the slow cooker and cook on low temp setting for 3 to 4 hours. 6. Serve warm.

Per Serving: Calories 298; Fat 21g; Sodium 708mg; Carbs 13g; Fibre 2g; Sugar 3g; Protein 14g

Vibrant Blueberry Crisp

Prep time: 10 minutes | Cook time: 3-4 hours | Serves: 8

5 tablespoons coconut oil, melted, divided

590g blueberries

20g plus 2 tablespoons granulated erythritol

95g ground pecans

1 teaspoon baking soda

½ teaspoon ground cinnamon

2 tablespoons coconut milk

1 egg

1. Lightly grease a slow cooker with 1 tablespoon of the coconut oil. 2. Add the blueberries and 2 tablespoons of erythritol to the slow cooker. 3. In a bowl, stir the remaining erythritol, ground pecans, baking soda, and cinnamon until well mixed. 4. Add the coconut milk, egg, and remaining coconut oil, and stir until coarse crumbs form. 5. Top the blueberry with the pecan mixture. 6. Cover the slow cooker and cook on low temp setting for 3 to 4 hours. 7. Serve warm.

Per Serving: Calories 160; Fat 15g; Sodium 66mg; Carbs 6g; Fibre 0g; Sugar 1g; Protein 2g

Pound Cake

Prep time: 10 minutes | Cook time: 5-6 hours | Serves: 8

1 tablespoon coconut oil

200g almond flour

35g granulated erythritol

½ teaspoon cream of tartar

Pinch salt

220g butter, melted

5 eggs

2 teaspoons pure vanilla extract

1. Lightly grease an 20-by-10cm loaf pan with the coconut oil. 2. In a bowl, stir the almond flour, erythritol, cream of tartar, and salt, until well mixed. 3. In a bowl, whisk the butter, eggs, and vanilla. 4. Add the wet ingredients to the dry ingredients and stir to combine. 5. Transfer the batter to the loaf pan. 6. Place the loaf pan in the slow cooker. 7. Cover and cook until a toothpick end in the centre comes out clean, about 5 to 6 hours on low temp setting. 8. Serve warm.

Per Serving: Calories 164; Fat 13g; Sodium 126mg; Carbs 11g; Fibre 2g; Sugar 1g; Protein 5g

Lemon Cake

Prep time: 10 minutes | Cook time: 6 hours | Serves: 8

Coconut oil, for greasing

200g almond flour

15g erythritol

2 teaspoons baking powder

3 eggs

110g unsalted butter or Ghee (here), melted and cooled slightly

120g double cream

Grated zest and juice of 2 lemons

1. Grease the slow cooker with coconut oil. 2. In a medium bowl, mix the almond flour, erythritol, and baking powder. 3. In a bowl, beat the eggs, then whisk in the butter, double cream, lemon zest, and lemon juice. 4. Add the dry ingredients to the wet ingredients. Stir to mix well. Transfer the batter to the and spread evenly with a rubber spatula. 5. Pour the glaze over the cake batter. Cover and cook for 6 hours on low temp setting or 3 hours on high. Serve warm or at room temperature.

Per Serving: Calories 285; Fat 24g; Sodium 188mg; Carbs 9g; Fibre 4g; Sugar 2g; Protein 9g

Ginger Cake With Whipped Cream

Prep time: 10 minutes | Cook time: 3 hours | Serves: 10

For the Cake

110g unsalted butter, melted, plus more for coating the slow cooker

225g almond flour

25g erythritol

2 tablespoons coconut flour

1½ tablespoons ground ginger

1 tablespoon unsweetened cocoa powder

2 teaspoons baking powder

1½ teaspoons ground cinnamon

½ teaspoon ground cloves

¼ teaspoon fine sea salt

4 eggs, lightly beaten

160g double cream

1 teaspoon pure vanilla extract

For the Whipped Cream

240g double cream

½ teaspoon stevia powder

1 teaspoon pure vanilla extract

1. Coat the slow cooker with butter. 2. In a bowl, mix the almond flour, erythritol, coconut flour, ginger, cocoa powder, baking powder, cinnamon, cloves, and sea salt. 3. Add butter, eggs, double cream, and vanilla. Mix and transfer to the slow cooker. 4. Cover and cook for 3 hours on low temp setting. Serve warm with whipped cream.

Per Serving: Calories 125; Fat 2g; Sodium 5mg; Carbs 23.46g; Fibre 0.9g; Sugar 13.09g; Protein 5.89g

Classical Vanilla Cheesecake

Prep time: 15 minutes | Cook time: 4 hours | Serves: 8

For the Crust

95g toasted walnuts, ground to a meal

1 egg, lightly beaten

2 tablespoons coconut oil, melted

For the Filling

2 eggs

2 (200g) packages cream cheese, at room temperature

60g double cream

1 teaspoon stevia powder

240ml water

2 teaspoons pure vanilla extract

15g erythritol

1 tablespoon coconut flour

½ teaspoon stevia powder

To make the crust: 1. In a bowl, mix the walnut meal, egg, coconut oil, and stevia powder. Press the mixture into the bottom of a baking pan that fits into slow cooker (make sure there is room to lift the pan out). An oval baking dish, round cake pan, or loaf pan could all work, depending on the size and shape of slow cooker. 2. Pour the water into the slow cooker. Place the pan in the cooker.

To make the filling: 1. In a bowl, beat the eggs, then beat in the cream cheese, double cream, vanilla, erythritol, coconut flour, and stevia powder. Pour the mixture over the crust. Cover and cook for 4 hours on low temp setting hours on low temp setting or 2 hours on high. 2. When finished, turn off the cooker and let the cheesecake sit inside until cooled to room temperature, up to 3 hours. 3. Remove the pan from the slow cooker and refrigerate until chilled, about 2 hours more. Serve chilled.

Per Serving: Calories 511; Fat 22.5g; Sodium 3036mg; Carbs 1g; Fibre 0.1g; Sugar 0.1g; Protein 66.7g

Sweet Lentil with Coconut

Prep time: 10 minutes | Cook time: 2 hours | Serves: 4

190g red lentils, rinsed well

360ml water, heated to boiling

155g dark brown sugar

1 (375g) can whole coconut milk

½ teaspoon ground cardamom

4 teaspoons toasted coconut

4 teaspoons pistachio nuts, finely chopped

1. Mix the red lentils, water, and brown sugar in a slow cooker. Cover the slow cooker and cook on low temp setting for 2 hours. 2. Uncover and stir in the coconut milk and ground cardamom. Re-cover and cook for one hour. 3. Serve topped with toasted coconut and pistachio nuts.

Per Serving: Calories 331; Fat 1.76g; Sodium 60mg; Carbs 55g; Fibre 5.6g; Sugar 24g; Protein 15.66g

Classical Chocolate Cake

Prep time: 10 minutes | Cook time: 1-2 hours | Serves: 8

250g plain flour

400g sugar

75g unsweetened cocoa powder

1¾ teaspoons baking powder

1¾ teaspoons baking soda

300ml regular or low-fat milk

2 eggs

120ml vegetable oil

300ml water

1. In a bowl, mix all the dry ingredients. In another bowl, mix all the wet ingredients. 2. Spray a slow cooker with cooking spray. Combine the dry and wet ingredients just until moistened and pour into the slow cooker. 3. Cover and cook on high temp setting heat for 1–2 hours. Remove cake from slow cooker and let cool.

Per Serving: Calories 326; Fat 15.4g; Sodium 2048mg; Carbs 4g; Fibre 0.8g; Sugar 1.4g; Protein 28.2g

Carrot Cake

Prep time: 10 minutes | Cook time: 2 hours | Serves: 8

185g plain flour

½ teaspoon baking soda

1 teaspoon baking powder

¼ teaspoon salt

¾ teaspoon cinnamon

¼ teaspoon ground cloves

⅛ teaspoon freshly grated nutmeg

2 eggs or 2 mashed bananas

150g sugar

75g margarine

60ml water

120g carrots, grated

25g raisins

60g chopped walnuts

1. In a mixing bowl, add the flour, baking soda, baking powder, cloves, salt, cinnamon, and nutmeg. Stir to combine. 2. In a food processor, add the eggs or bananas, sugar, and margarine. Process to cream. Scrape into the flour mixture. 3. Pour in the water and add the grated carrots to the mixing bowl. Stir and fold to combine all ingredients. Fold in the raisins and nuts. 4. Spray the slow cooker with cooking spray. Add the carrot cake batter and use a spatula to spread it evenly in the crock. Cover the slow cooker and cook on low temp setting for 2 hours until cake is firm in the centre.

Per Serving: Calories 173; Fat 7.4g; Sodium 1538mg; Carbs 7g; Fibre 1.4g; Sugar 1.6g; Protein 19g

Creamy Custard

Prep time: 10 minutes | Cook time: 2-4 hours | Serves: 4

Cooking spray

3 eggs

480ml whole milk

20g powdered erythritol sweetener of choice

½ teaspoon vanilla extract

⅛ teaspoon nutmeg

1. Coat a slow cooker with cooking spray. 2. In a bowl, mix the eggs, whole milk, erythritol, vanilla, and nutmeg. Spread the mixture evenly in the bottom of the slow cooker. 3. Place a paper towel between the slow cooker and the lid to cut down on any condensation that develops. Cook on low temp setting for 2 to 4 hours or on high for 1 to 2 hours until a toothpick inserted into the centre and comes out clean. 4. Let cool before serving.

Per Serving: Calories: 235; Fat: 16g; Carbohydrates: 14g; Fibre: 0g; Protein: 9g; Sodium: 127mg

Dates Pudding

Prep time: 10 minutes | Cook time: 4 hours | Serves: 8

370g dates, pitted and snipped

1½ teaspoons baking soda

400ml boiling water

410g dark brown sugar, packed

110g unsalted butter, softened

¼ teaspoon salt

Cooking spray

Whipped cream

3 eggs

2 teaspoons vanilla extract

440g plain flour

4 teaspoons baking powder

1. Add the dates to a mixing bowl and toss them with the baking soda. Pour the boiling water over the dates. Set aside. 2. Add the brown sugar and butter to a food processor. Process to cream them, and then continue to process while you add the eggs and vanilla. 3. Use a spatula to scrape the brown sugar mixture into the bowl with the dates. Stir to mix. 4. Add the flour, baking powder, and salt to a bowl; stir to mix. 5. Fold into the date and brown sugar mixture. 6. Treat a slow cooker with cooking spray. Pour the batter into the slow cooker. Cover the slow cooker and cook on low temp setting for 4 hours or until the centre of the pudding cake is set but still moist. 7. Serve warm with quick sauce and a dollop of whipped cream if desired.

Per Serving: Calories 692; Fat 12.71g; Sodium 393mg; Carbs 136g; Fibre 6g; Sugar 83.21g; Protein 15.66g

Chocolaty Crème Brûlée

Prep time: 10 minutes | Cook time: 3 hours | Serves: 4

480ml evaporated milk, regular or low-fat

2½ tablespoons cocoa powder

½ teaspoon vanilla extract

4 egg yolks

100g sugar

2 packed tablespoons brown sugar

240ml water

1. In a bowl, whisk the evaporated milk, cocoa, vanilla, egg yolks, and sugar until the sugar dissolves. Pour the mixture into a small pan and bring it to a boil. Remove the pan from the heat and allow the mixture to cool. 2. Divide it among 4 (125 – 150g) grill-safe ramekins. Pour 240ml of water into the bottom of an oval slow cooker. Place the ramekins in the water. Cook on high for 3 hours or until the custard is set. 3. Sprinkle each Crème Brûlée with ½ tablespoon brown sugar. Place them under the griller and grill until the sugar caramelizes.

Per Serving: Calories 101; Fat 4.47g; Sodium 31mg; Carbs 12.47g; Fibre 0.5g; Sugar 11.26g; Protein 3.58g

Crunchy Apple Brown Betty

Prep time: 10 minutes | Cook time: 2 hours | Serves: 6

Cooking spray

380g cubed apples

1 tablespoon lemon juice

1 tablespoon sugar

½ teaspoon cinnamon

½ teaspoon ground ginger

¼ teaspoon nutmeg

¼ teaspoon allspice

95g 1cm bread cubes

1. Grease a slow cooker with cooking spray. Add the apples, lemon juice, sugar, and spices. Stir. Cook on high temp setting for 2 hours. 2. Preheat oven to 120°C. Spread the bread cubes in a single layer on a baking sheet. Bake until browned, about 8 minutes. 3. Sprinkle the toasted bread cubes over the apples. Cook on high temp for 10 minutes prior to serving.

Per Serving: Calories 68; Fat 0.51g; Sodium 51mg; Carbs 15.73g; Fibre 2g; Sugar 8.57g; Protein 1.11g

Blueberry Muffin

Prep time: 15 minutes | Cook time: 4-6 hours | Serves: 10

Cooking spray

300g almond flour

120g low fat plain Greek yogurt

10g powdered erythritol sweetener of choice

3 eggs

2 to 3 teaspoons grated lemon zest

1½ teaspoons baking powder

1 teaspoon vanilla extract

½ teaspoon baking soda

¼ teaspoon salt

150g fresh or frozen blueberries

1. Coat a slow cooker with cooking spray. 2. In a bowl, mix the almond flour, yogurt, erythritol, eggs, lemon zest, baking powder, vanilla, baking soda, and salt until well blended. Carefully fold in the blueberries. 3. Pour the batter into the slow cooker. 4. Place a paper towel between the slow cooker and the lid to cut down on any condensation that develops. Cook on low temp setting for 4 to 6 hours until a toothpick inserted in the centre and comes out clean.

Per Serving: Calories 77; Fat 3.37g; Sodium 162mg; Carbs 8.51g; Fibre 0.5g; Sugar 7g; Protein 3.48g

Homemade Pecan Cookie

Prep time: 10 minutes | Cook time: 4-6 hours | Serves: 8

Cooking spray

125g almond flour

15g powdered erythritol sweetener of choice

40g chopped pecans

1 egg

5 tablespoons unsalted butter, at room temperature

1 tablespoon coconut flour

1 teaspoon baking powder

½ teaspoon vanilla extract

1. Coat a slow cooker with cooking spray. 2. In a bowl, mix the almond flour, erythritol, pecans, egg, butter, coconut flour, baking powder, and vanilla until well blended. Pour the batter into the slow cooker. 3. Place a paper towel between the slow cooker and the lid to cut down on any condensation that develops. 4. Cook on low temp setting for 4 to 6 hours or on high for 2 to 3 hours until a toothpick inserted in the centre and comes out clean.

Per Serving: Calories 151; Fat 9.07g; Sodium 20mg; Carbs 17.25g; Fibre 0.4g; Sugar 15.55g; Protein 1.84g

Pumpkin Pie

Prep time: 10 minutes | Cook time: 2-4 hours | Serves: 4

Cooking spray

1 (375g) can pumpkin purée (without salt)

4 eggs, beaten

120ml whole milk

10g powdered erythritol sweetener of choice

1½ teaspoons vanilla

1 teaspoon pumpkin pie spice

½ teaspoon salt

1. Coat a slow cooker with cooking spray. 2. In a bowl, mix the pumpkin, eggs, milk, vanilla, erythritol, pumpkin pie spice, and salt. Spread the mixture evenly in the bottom of the slow cooker. 3. Place a paper towel between the slow cooker and the lid to cut down on any condensation that develops. Cook on low temp setting for 2 to 4 hours or on high for 1 to 2 hours.

Per Serving: Calories 342; Fat 16.45g; Sodium 414mg; Carbs 33.82g; Fibre 5.6g; Sugar 16.15g; Protein 15.46g

Delicious Strawberry Ricotta Cheesecake

Prep time: 10 minutes | Cook time: 2-4 hours | Serves: 4

Cooking spray

480g part-skim ricotta cheese

120g Strawberry Sauce

2 eggs

1 tablespoon plus 2 teaspoons powdered erythritol sweetener of choice

1 teaspoon vanilla extract

1. Coat a slow cooker with cooking spray. 2. In a bowl, mix the ricotta, strawberry sauce, eggs, erythritol, and vanilla until well blended. Pour the mixture into the slow cooker. 3. Place a paper towel between the slow cooker and the lid to cut down on any condensation that develops. Cook on low temp setting for 2 to 4 hours or on high for 1 to 2 hours until a toothpick inserted into the centre comes out clean.

Per Serving: Calories 249; Fat 14.68g; Sodium 174mg; Carbs 9.45g; Fibre 0.4g; Sugar 2.7g; Protein 18.73g

Green Tea Pudding

Prep time: 10 minutes | Cook time: 1½ hours | Serves: 6

480ml fat-free evaporated milk

1 teabag green tea

40g small pearl tapioca

1 teaspoon matcha or green tea powder

100g sugar

1 egg

1. Heat evaporated milk in a saucepan just until it barely simmers. Remove from heat and add teabag. Let steep for 2 minutes. 2. Pour the milk mixture, tapioca, matcha or green tea powder and sugar into a slow cooker. 3. Whisk until the sugar dissolves. Cook for 1½ hours on high. Stir in the egg. Cook for an half hour on low. Serve warm.

Per Serving: Calories 105; Fat 1.76g; Sodium 60mg; Carbs 18g; Fibre 0.1g; Sugar 12.46g; Protein 4.3g

Creamy Chocolate Nut Cheesecake

Prep time: 15 minutes | Cook time: 4 hours | Serves: 8

For the Crust

95g macadamia nuts, ground to a meal

1 egg, lightly beaten

2 tablespoons coconut oil, melted

1 teaspoon stevia powder

240g water

For the Filling

150g unsweetened chocolate, chopped

2 eggs

2 (200g) packages cream cheese, at room

temperature

60g coconut cream

1 tablespoon coconut flour

1 teaspoon pure vanilla extract

15g erythritol

½ teaspoon stevia powder

30g coarsely chopped macadamia nuts

To make the crust: 1. In a bowl, stir the macadamia nut meal, egg, coconut oil, and stevia powder. 2. Press the mixture into the bottom of a baking pan that fits into slow cooker (make sure there is room on the sides so you can lift the pan out). An oval baking dish, round cake pan, or loaf pan could all work, depending on the size and shape of slow cooker. 3. Pour the water into the slow cooker. Place the pan in the cooker.

TO make the filling: 1. In a microwave-safe bowl, heat the chocolate in the microwave for 1 minute on high. Stir and then microwave in 30-second intervals, stirring in between, until the chocolate is melted and smooth. Set aside. 2. In a bowl, beat the eggs, then beat in the cream cheese, coconut cream, coconut flour, vanilla, erythritol, and stevia powder. 3. Stir in the chocolate until well incorporated. Pour the mixture over the crust. Cover and cook for 4 hours on low temp setting or 2 hours on high temp. 4. When finished, turn off the slow cooker and let the cheesecake sit inside until cooled to room temperature, up to 3 hours. 5. Remove the pan from the slow cooker and refrigerate until chilled, about 2 hours more. 6. Sprinkle the macadamia nuts over the top and serve chilled.

Per Serving: Calories 367; Fat 24g; Sodium 240mg; Carbs 12g; Fibre 1g; Sugar 2g; Protein 8g

Prep time: 10 minutes| Cook time: 2-2½ hours| Serves: 12

Nonstick cooking spray

100g unsweetened cocoa powder

125g oat flour, whole-wheat pastry flour, or plain flour

120g unsweetened dried cherries

40g ground flaxseed

2 teaspoons baking powder

¼ teaspoon salt

2 tablespoons extra-virgin olive oil

1 egg

2 egg whites

1 tablespoon vanilla extract

100g granulated sugar

120g nonfat vanilla Greek yogurt

180ml low-fat or fat-free milk, or plant-based milk, divided

1. Lightly coat the slow cooker with the cooking spray. 2. In a bowl, whisk the cocoa powder, flour, dried cherries, flaxseed, baking powder, and salt. 3. In a bowl, whisk the oil, egg, egg whites, and vanilla. Add in the sugar, yogurt, and 60ml of milk, mixing thoroughly until no lumps remain. Add the flour mixture and remaining milk, stirring until just combined and incorporated. 4. Spread the batter in the slow cooker. Cover the slow cooker and cook on low temp setting for 2 to 2½ hours until the centre no longer looks moist and feels barely firm to the touch. Remove the lid, turn off the slow cooker, and cool the cake in the ceramic bowl for 15 to 20 minutes before carefully turning it out onto a wire rack to cool completely. 5. Cut into 12 slices and enjoy.

Per Serving: Calories 181; Fat 15g; Sodium 36mg; Carbs 10g; Fibre 4g; Sugar 1g; Protein 6g

Conclusion

As the name implies, slow cookers are kitchen tools that take their time to prepare meals. An easy-to-use, portable electric device that is common in modern kitchens is the slow cooker. Slow cookers provide several benefits. "All day cooking without seeing" is what it is. They are inexpensive to run and an excellent technique to soften less costly and harder meat pieces (shoulder, round, and chuck). Foods have more taste when they are cooked slowly. One-pot dinners, soups, stews, and casseroles are just a few of the many dishes that may be prepared in a slow cooker. Compared to an oven, a slow cooker consumes less power.

Appendix Recipes Index

Delicious Wild Mushroom Risotto 36

E

Easy Breakfast Barley   12
Easy Dried Beans Stew   32
Easy Pho Soup   80

F

Flank Steak Tacos   54

G

Garlic Veggie with Lentils   35
Garlicky Button Mushrooms   23
Ginger Cake With Whipped Cream 88
Gingered Chicken Thighs   48
Green Beans & Mushroom
Casserole   24
Green Tea Pudding   95

H

Healthy Blueberry-Coconut Quinoa 10
Healthy Farro   38
Healthy Kung Pao Chicken   42
Hearty Beef Brisket with Sweet
Potatoes   64
Herbed Lentils   38
Herbed Meatloaf   13
Homemade Pecan Cookie   93
Hot Beef Bourguignon   68
Hot Beef Chili with Corn Chips   66

I

Indian Chicken and Chickpea Curry 50

J

Japanese Triple Pork Soup   84

K

Kale & Bacon Stew   22

L

Lemon Cake   88
Lemon Garlicky Asparagus   29
Lima Bean and Veggie Casserole 33
Lime Chicken Avocado Soup   83
Lime Chicken with Guacamole
Cream Sauce   40

Lime-Coconut Red Beans with Rice 34

M

Maple-Pecan Brussels   20
Mediterranean-Style Eggs   14
Mexican-style Lasagna   26
Mixed Beans and Barely Soup   73
Mushroom & Wild Rice Medley
with Pecans   34
Mushroom Burritos   30

N

Navy Bean Soup and Ham Soup 72

O

One-Pot Whole Chicken with
Thyme   44
Overnight Oatmeal with Raisins 16

P

Pecan Barley Porridge with
Blueberries   16
Peppercorn Vegetable Stock   69
Pork Loin with Creamy Gravy   61
Pork Loin with Gingery Cream
Sauce   63
Pound Cake   87
Pumpkin and Yogurt Soup   22
Pumpkin Pie   94

Q

Quinoa and Vegetables Casserole 35
Quinoa with Walnuts and Apples 15

R

Refreshing Salsa Verde Chicken 41

S

Sausage and Kale Soup 75
Sausage Egg Scramble   19
Smoked Salmon & Asparagus
Quiche 15
Soft Buttery Coconut Bread   12
Spiced Chicken 46
Spiced Pork Belly with Brussels
Sprouts & Turnips   59
Spicy Beef Goulash   57

Spicy Beef Short Ribs   53
Spicy Black Bean Soup 72
Spicy Mushroom and Tofu Soup 84
Spicy Teriyaki Chicken 49
Sweet & Sour White Beans   33
Sweet & Spicy Pinto Beans   32
Sweet Chicken and Broccoli   44
Sweet Lentil with Coconut   89
Swiss Steak and Carrot Stew   65

T

Tangy Balsamic Roast Beef   57
Tangy Barley and Mushroom   39
Tangy Beef and Olive   62
Tangy Beef Bone Stock 76
Tangy Chocolate Fondue   85
Tangy Mustard-Herb Pork Chops 61
Tangy Orange Chicken   47
Tasty Beef & Mushroom Meatballs 67
Tasty Sweet Potatoes   20
Tender Steak Stew   60
Thai-Style Green Curry with Tofu
& Vegetables   24
Tofu and Mushroom Curry with Nuts 23
Traditional Blackberry Cobbler 86
Tropical Lemongrass Pork   59
Tuna and Mushroom Noodles   27

V

Vibrant Blueberry Crisp 87

W

Warm Vanilla Pear Crisp   86
Warm Vegetable Stock   78

Printed in Great Britain
by Amazon

20735505R00062